THE GURU'S RULES FOR

LOCAL ADVERTISING

IT'S ALL ABOUT

MEASURABLE RESULTS

BY DON FITZGIBBONS

CREDITS

EDITING HELP FROM

Mike Fitzgibbons - Erin Palumbo- Meghan Hamilton

Robin Renna

ART WORK

Jamie Fitzgibbons

CONSIDERABLE INSPIRATION

Jim Doyle - Og Mandino

Douglas Sullivan

TOLERANCE

Jan Fitzgibbons

PUBLISHING SUPERVISION

Shawn Fitzgibbons

ALL STORIES IN THIS BOOK
ARE TRUE.

SOME NAMES AND LOCATIONS
HAVE BEEN CHANGED TO
PROTECT ME.

TABLE OF CONTENTS

THE MIND OF THE GURU: A FORWARD

BY NATHAN PALUMBO
FORMER NASA ROCKET SCIENTIST

Much like the medieval Knights of the Round Table in search of the Holy Grail, the Guru of Ads has been on a noble quest on behalf of local advertisers. His mission: to eradicate pitiful, wasteful, ineffective local advertising and make ads that deliver measurable results.

For decades, the Guru has traveled extensively. He first created advertising campaigns in the northeast then consulted over 3,000 local advertisers in hundreds of cities nationwide in his selfless search for measurable results. Along the way, the U.S. State Department hired him to help advance advertising in Bosnia, Zimbabwe, Yugoslavia, Romania and Nepal.

As he tells his story, "About ten years ago, just after I returned from Nepal, something snapped and I decided to launch a personal crusade against ineffective local advertising. Now I hope to share everything I have learned with you in this book." When he hears about local advertising that fails, he bristles and cries, "It's time to stop this madness."

If you agree, you are about to embark on a voyage of discovery into the 14 Rules of the Guru, with promise of more measurable results more often for your business. Here is the best news of all, it is *not* rocket science.

PREFACE

In the next chapters I will share with you my years of hard-earned, real-life experiences about the quirky world of advertising. The lessons in this book will help you achieve real, measurable results. In fact, I make the bold claim that businesses that follow my advice can increase their success rate dramatically.

Some of you may be doubtful and even thinking that reading this will be a waste of your time. Not to worry, you can always get your money back if you saved the receipt and you can find me.

Then again, you might be convinced that I really do have the experience and knowledge to lead you to improve your advertising and help you get the measurable results you deserve without increasing your advertising budget. Even more important, I want you to achieve a return on your advertising budget that makes you happy.

Alas, as you know by now, this does not happen often enough. It's a crime against your bottom line! So why do we accept failure?

Some of you look at advertising with an almost religious faith. You put up a certain amount of money every month and hope you're backing something that will pay off eventually. That's faith-based advertising. For years it worked. Let us say it worked up until the 1980's and 1990's. This was the accepted strategy back then when there were fewer media outlets and no Internet. Back then you could reach a huge audience with an ad in the daily newspaper. Back then just being on TV meant you were a player. Those days are gone forever!

A Madison Avenue ad agency king once said, "I know that 50 percent of my advertising works - I just don't know what 50 percent it is!" It was an acceptable strategy back then to cast money to the winds and assume some of it worked. Those days are also long gone.

Another reason we accept failure is due to pure confusion. Things are changing so fast that it boggles the mind. Marketing is undergoing a sea of change, and as the technology of the country changes, so have the strategies that make local advertising work. Many copywriting or media placement strategies from just a year ago are simply no longer valid. The web affects everything. We will discuss all of this in the next chapters so you can better adapt to this new world order of advertising.

Be advised, however, that the focus in this book is on electronic advertising in radio, television, cable television, plus the effect of the Internet on advertising. There will also be some valuable advice on other major media like billboards, newspapers, yellow pages and direct mail. There will only be passing references to the insignificant players like mobile billboards, movie theater advertising, restaurant placemat ads, bus signs, bench signs, yearbooks and church bulletins etc.

However, urinal ads in men's rooms at bars will get a surprising vote of confidence.

HOW I BECAME A GURU
OF LOCAL ADVERTISING

First, let me make it clear, I am a self-appointed Guru. I was a "military brat" and have lived all over the map. I have never been a Buddhist; however, I did receive a rather draconian education from well-intentioned Catholic brothers and nuns from the 2nd through 12th grades. As a University of Wisconsin student in the 60s, known at that time for its liberal left-wing ideology, I joined in the revolt against the powers that be and turned to beer for spiritual comfort.

In developing my "Guru" status, I copied the strategy used by Napoleon when he declared himself Emperor of France in 1872. With papist bishops, Lady Josephine and the masses in attendance, he crowned himself in Notre Dame Cathedral. A brilliant maneuver, which in today's advertising terms we call "positioning" or "branding."

My own self coronation occurred in bleaker circumstances. It was the winter of 1999.

Alone in a hotel room in a depleted neighborhood in Manchester, New Hampshire, I realized I was just one of the thousands of businessmen who called themselves advertising consultants. Desperately needing to break out of the pack, with Jerry Springer as my silent TV witness, I made the decision to anoint myself the one, the only and the unique "Guru of Ads!"

At that point, my resume hardly conformed to your typical business type. After college, I was a backseat navigator flying F-4 Phantoms in Vietnam and later baby sitting nuclear bombs to help win the cold war in England. Then came jobs as a stock market broker, a lobster peddler, a car salesman and a dog kennel owner with a side business renting out a 1933 Rolls Royce limo for weddings.

Finally about 1976 I started a 20-year career in radio advertising sales in small runty radio stations in small markets. Ah, but there was a silver lining in all those small stations.

Because I had no market ratings to sell to the big ad agencies, I was forced to rely on my own ideas in developing local ads that worked for mom and pop stores with smaller budgets. Simply put, my ads had to get results or I starved.

In that era, radio ratings were more important than marketing results. I was the odd sales duck, targeting the small orders, $500 here or $300 there. I certainly would have preferred to sell in Boston, Los Angeles or New York City, working the big businesses that spent big bucks on the big stations. But in my small markets, I was a small fish doing cartwheels to keep my clients happy.

Then the world began to change in my favor, in the form of accelerating media fragmentation. The proliferation in TV stations, cable channels, the Internet and various media outlets all took their toll in robbing the big stations of their market dominance. The daily newspaper made the endangered species list as Tyrannosaurus Printus. Even the big three television outlets, ABC, CBS and NBC, were affected. With the public tuning in to a greater variety of media choices, the question became how to wisely invest sales and advertising dollars, especially with diminishing results for advertisers.

Then I landed the job that truly anointed me as The Guru of Ads. I had just left a radio station in Southbridge,

Massachusetts, (population 26,734) and begun working with Jim Doyle, a national sales trainer. He claims he rescued me from Southbridge as an act of mercy. I think he was right. Working for Jim landed me in that hotel room in Manchester, New Hampshire, in the winter of 1999. His mercy would soon bear fruit.

Jim needed someone to go into nationwide media outlets, especially television and cable markets, to make sales calls on their local advertisers. Manchester was my first such outing. My mission was to help sell TV schedules and to create, write or rewrite TV commercials to increase their effectiveness. Many of my ideas increased sales results. I got to keep the job! The Guru had arrived!

Since then I have met with over 3,000 business owners and managers nationwide who advertise for every imaginable type of business. I have analyzed and evaluated thousands of ads. In doing so I have acquired knowledge that only a Guru possesses. I know a lot about what works and what doesn't when it comes to local advertising.

I am continuously amazed at the failure of most ads. As the evidence mounted that an excessive failure rate was a nationwide phenomena, I knew I was on to something bigger than I could have possibly imagined. Finally, armed with enough of my own data, I sat down and did the math. Amazingly, 65 percent of the local advertisements that I studied failed!

Owners and managers of car dealerships, furniture stores, bakeries, hair salons, health clubs, tattoo parlors, lawyers, banks, travel agencies, restaurants, hospitals, candy stores and local retail mainstream stores told me over and over: most of their advertising failed to produce a measurable result.

The net effect on the entire advertising industry seemed to be equally disturbing. With ineffective advertisements, businesses either cancelled their ads or were forced to stumble like blind mice from one media outlet to the other, in search of results, like medieval knights in search of the Holy Grail.

Sales reps were equally traumatized. They fought the cancellation enemy and usually lost, often spending months closing sales which resulted in meager results when the ads finally aired. Something needed to be done.

RULE ONE:

IF IT DOESN'T WORK, IT IS A BAD AD

We usually pass judgment on our advertising based solely on how it looks or sounds. Yet in advertising, the fact that we love or hate a particular commercial *has no bearing on how good or bad it is.*

For example, here is a real commercial, broadcast of course, with the appropriate sound effects:

Radio Announcer: Imagine for a moment, the middle of the night, you're awakened from a sound sleep, a strange sound, the clock reads 2:14.

Narrator in a deep nervous voice:

The sound which woke you is disturbing,

A muted *Clump* like a heavy footstep.

Your ears strain for more.

Clumppp

There it is again, just beyond your door.

Clumppppp

It is very big, very heavy.

Clumpppppppp

And now … oh god, you can hear…….breathing!

Breathing in …*Uhhuuuuuhhhhhh…*

Then breathing out… *Whhhhooooohhhhhh*

And you smell its odor,

A dirty foul stench that reeks of danger.

Panicky you fumble for the phone,

Too late!

The door shatters,

Craaassssssshhhhhhhhhhhhhhhh!

Radio Announcer: To find out what happens next in the latest William Knong thriller *The Fog of Terror*, visit the

Maine Bookstore at the Portland Mall, on sale in hardcover for $19.99, for a limited time. Maine Booksellers: If it's in print, we've got it or we'll get it for you!

Now, what you just read was a **60**-second radio commercial.

When I first heard that ad, read in an evil, devil-like voice, accompanied by the clumping footsteps, the breathing intruder and the crashing door, I thought it was one of the best radio ads I had ever heard.

The copywriter was Dave Body of Body & Company Advertising, an eclectic ad agency populating the newly renovated and very hip downtown Portland, Maine waterfront in the 1980s. I was then a rookie radio sales rep in Dave's office and I told him how much I had liked the commercial.

Dave's reply shocked me. Even now I remember his exact blunt reply, "That ad was horrible. Awful."

Right then, Dave's words began to lay the groundwork for this book and specifically for this chapter. The lesson was simple.

If an ad fails to produce results for the client, it is a bad ad!

He continued, "That ad produced no results. It sold no books. It created no extra traffic in the store. Therefore it was a bad ad." No matter what I thought of its entertainment value, no matter if the ad even won every award at the Maine Addy Awards Ceremony, it was still a bad ad.

Like everyone, I had committed the most common of errors. We judge commercials based on our preferences, tastes, values, likes and dislikes. But remember the bottom line; all that matters are the results. In other words, what happens to sales when the ad hits the air?

Let's take the opposite end of the spectrum and take a look at an ad campaign that ran for three years on television in Charleston, North Carolina, a few years ago.

The client was a small tire company.

Someone came up with the idea of doing a parody of the Michelin Baby. You know, the cute little kid we saw going "wheeeee" and giggling as he slides along inside a Michelin tire on a ski slope?

But instead of a cute baby they substituted a 400-pound, half-naked, hunka-chub man in a diaper inside a tractor-trailer tire. It was grossssss!

You have already met him. His picture is right at the beginning of this chapter. Tell me honestly if you think Fat Louie was a good tire spokesperson. Do you think he helped sell tires or not?

On TV, he looked even worse. You could actually see fat bouncing up and down on his chest, not the most appealing visual sight.

But remember the bottom line.

Sure, Fat Louie was in bad taste. Women especially hated him, but stop right there. It doesn't matter what we think. What matters are results. Before we praise or condemn the ad we need to know if it generated a measurable increase in tire sales!

Fat Louie sold a lot of tires for that little tire store. Admittedly not many professional working moms visited the store, but it generated enough interest among other viewers, who loved the ad and bought enough tires to make Fat Louie a grand slam success!

So it was a great ad. A brilliant ad! It delivered **measurable results**, the ultimate outcome for the tire store, for the TV station running the ads and for the sales rep who sold the schedule.

A good ad produces measurable results. But it if doesn't work, it is bad!

Who likes it or dislikes it is of no consequence whatsoever.

The quality of the production is of no consequence.

The only thing that matters is the result.

I offer as further proof a survey which appears periodically in *USA Today*.

USA Today surveys people's like or dislike of ads appearing on national TV. Astoundingly, the most **popular** ads were liked a lot by only 21 percent of the respondents. And 21 percent was a good score. It is worth repeating. If 21 percent of those surveyed really like an ad that is a home run.

Sweet mother of pearl! That means 79 percent were not crazy about the ad and yet the ad still can get results?

Indeed it does!

Sure there are exceptions.

The Aflac duck, for example, scores a much higher than average rating as a commercial people like to watch. Come on, admit it, you love it! Aflacccccc! Not surprisingly, it has been a big success. But the duck is the exception.

Let us now examine the dark side of the survey. The ads that are most disliked. Surely they fail. Here are a couple to consider.

Do you recall the Capital One Barbarian Visigoths ("What's in your wallet?") and their vile spokesman, Mr. No?

Despite being ranked as one of the most disliked commercials, the people at Capital One tell us it was a huge success.

As one of their execs said, "The Visigoths took us from 'Capitol Who?' to become one of the top names in the credit card industry."

More recently we have Head On. Apply directly to the forehead. Apply directly to the forehead. Apply directly to the forehead. People hate it. People buy the product. Great ad!

Ok. Let's forget about our likes and dislikes, and focus only on what you can do to make your advertising work.

But to make sure you read carefully, let me add a note about blame. I have a mantra about blame that reads like this: "The fish rots from the head down." That means the ugly finger of blame gets pointed at the manager of the business buying the ads and guilty of injecting all their likes and dislikes, or it gets pointed at the managers of the media who refuse to intervene and allow ads, guaranteed to fail, to run.

RULE TWO:

DO YOUR DETECTIVE WORK

Thus far, we have established a significant basic premise: Only measurable results define a good ad. There will be an appendix at the end of the book to help you define measurable results. But right now, it's time to raise the obvious question. What do you do when you feel like the advertising is failing?

We usually start by blaming either the ad itself or the station that ran it.

Recently I fielded a request to review just such a TV ad. It was a horrid, wretched, awful, pathetic, worthless, useless waste of money. I describe the experience in such negative terms for one simple reason: The ad was failing to produce results of any kind despite a significant investment in money and airtime.

The obvious question was this: What went wrong and how do we fix it? Let's see what you think.

The commercial was for a local, non-profit foundation in a medium-sized, Midwest city. The funds from the foundation were used to help starving children. The cause was good and they were totally legitimate, with over 98 percent of donations going directly to the children's care.

The ad itself had an artistic look. Clearly the production crew had done a professional job. They used film. The music was of the inspirational variety you would hear in a spa or a marriage counselor's office – Yanni or Enya? The script was poetic and heart tugging with scenes of hungry, cute kids, accompanied by a brief postscript soliciting donations.

Yet the ad didn't produce results. Why? For starters, the name of the foundation was muddied. Worse, the viewer had no idea what they were specifically supposed to do if they did want to help the starving kids. By specifics, I mean things such as how much money a viewer should send, where to send it, what the money would be used for, why the money was needed now, and even where the foundation was located was difficult to determine from the ad. Crucial information was lost in the beauty of the ad itself.

So by applying Rule One, we are now correct to pass judgment and send this ad straight to advertising hell.

But what about that hollow what-do-I-do-next feeling? If looks, production, great voices and heart-tugging, emotional appeal combined with a generous broadcast schedule can't guarantee success, then what does?

That's why there are 14 rules in this book. In each, I will walk you through the basics of what causes ads to fail or succeed.

Our focus now is transforming bad ads into good ones. Later sections will help you create and judge ads that have never aired. But right now let's take one thing at a time.

To begin allow me to call upon those gurus of old who have shown me the way, the truth and the light. I share their wisdom with you. It is most important to make a distinction here; my best teachers have been great detectives, not great creators. Let me explain.

The best way to write and produce successful ads is to be a great detective rather than a brilliant creator.

This may surprise you. You may be thinking the best source of expertise in advertising would be from creative Madison Avenue types such as Hill Holiday, McCann Erickson, Chiat/Day, Young and Rubicom, The Bornstein Group and so on.

You may also be thinking that it was their creative genius that was solely responsible for successful ads such as the Geico gecko, "Tastes Great/ Less Filling," the Pillsbury Dough Boy, "Apply directly to the forehead," the Marlboro Man and the Travelocity gnome.

You may be surprised to know that the actual creative part of these ads, those catchy phrases or symbols, were developed at the end of a long and exhaustive sequence of detective work.

It's worth repeating. The actual creative part of these ads, those catchy phrases or symbols, were developed at the end of a long and exhaustive sequence of detective work.

It was not creative genius alone that made those ads work. They worked, because somebody did good, detailed, slogging detective work before the ad was created. That involves studies of demographics, traffic patterns, seasonal trends, market trends, perceptual studies, economic trending, consumer tastes and it often entails actual interviews, focus groups and exhaustive surveys.

Good ad agencies understand the value of detective work. They do it first. So should you. Before anyone writes one single word, he or she needs to investigate the client, their product and their services. So should you. They do focus groups. So should you. They examine the competition. So should you. They look at the real world. So should you.

Just like a real detective trying to collect the evidence to solve a crime, you should try to collect the information that will help you get the results you seek.

In fact, if you are the business owner or manager in charge of advertising, you may fall victim to the adage, "Can't see the forest for the trees." I would suggest you not only review each of the 14 Rules, but get out of town and do it from a distance.

Just as detectives don't make an arrest until they have solid evidence, you should not begin to write until you have a clear picture of things. Once the detective work is done, it is much easier to incorporate the creativity. Let's look back at a few of the national ads for clarification.

Years ago, one ad agency working for McDonald's discovered that few consumers knew what was inside a Big Mac. So people didn't buy them. The agency therefore focused on the ingredients and the creative department developed the jingle that allowed most of us to memorize them: "Two all-beef patties, special sauce, lettuce, cheese…." McDonald's sold billions of Big Macs after airing that ad.

Another case of detective work by an agency revealed their client, the American Family Life Assurance Company, had a problem with name recognition. Their studies showed that when the field sales force made calls on potential customers, only 9 percent knew they were a supplemental health insurance organization. The agency's detective work revealed that if name recognition increased, so would sales. The hand off to creative was a request to simply create name recognition. In the next year the Aflac duck took them to near 90-percent name recognition and the $60 million annual ad budget never increased. (They did shift most of it to dominate TV.) It just took detective work followed by a change in the creative to help gain dramatic success.

Being a good detective beats being creative.

Let's look at what it takes to be a good detective and then demonstrate how it relates to preparing an advertising campaign for your business on a local level. Let's review some of the best from the world of fiction. Hopefully, there is one character on this list you will recognize and relate to:

Nancy Drew

Inspector Closseau

Sherlock Holmes

Dick Tracey

Ace Ventura

Columbo

Perry Mason

Hercule Poirot

Joe Friday

Dog the Bounty Hunter

Here are the common denominators in all these detectives: They ask a lot of questions, think a lot and follow up on a lot of leads. These detectives usually spend a couple hundred pages in a book or the entire length of the TV show or movie asking questions and thinking, while tracking down leads until they get one suspect.

Just imagine what would happen if the detective tried to cram in a whole list of suspects like we do in our ads. The great detective stands before the judge, jury, TV cameras or newspaper reporters and announces:

"I am convinced beyond a shadow of a doubt that we have solved this case. The guilty culprit is no other than one of these: Mrs. John Jones or Mr. Harry Cleaver, or possibly a certain Mr. Homer Watson, or likely it was the late Johnny Jones or his wife Patricia. I have arrested them all!"

We have all played the detective game Clue. What would happen if one of the players stood and said:

"I hereby accuse Mrs. White, or maybe it was Col Mustard, and if not them, Miss Scarlet or Professor Plumb of the murder. And I suspect the one who did it used the knife or the gun, or maybe the rope, but certainly it happened in the Billiard Room or else it was the Kitchen."

Both of those examples are laughable in real life because they are laundry lists with no detective work done to single out the most likely suspect.

You may well laugh and say, "What does this have to do with my advertising?" Let's look at commercial campaigns using a laundry list. See if this strikes you as being no different than accusing multiple suspects of a crime:

At Harry's Used Car Center, we specialize in the best used cars, the best used trucks and the best used SUVs. Not only that, but we also have a selection of low-mileage cars with full warranty or high-mileage cars sold 'as is' for a lot less.

You will find full service, including oil changes, tune ups and car-detailing services provided by our friendly staff of local family members who have been helping local folks with nighttime hours and weekend service by appointment.

Presenting a laundry list of services for a business in a commercial is just as bad as presenting the judge in a trial with a laundry list of potential suspects. Nothing stands out. When a commercial airs with a laundry list, it usually fails.

My personal favorite detective of all time was Joe Friday from the radio show (yes, I'm that old to have heard a radio show) and also in the 1950s TV series *Dragnet*. Some of you may remember the great punch line from the show, "There's a thousand stories in the city…dum dum dum, dumm…..this is one of them!"

The format was pretty simple. There was a crime and Joe Friday spent most of his time on the radio or TV doing basic detective work. He had a great line that I have copied and used over and over in my work. Whenever he was asking questions about the crime and the person being interviewed started to drift into speculation or emotional statements, Joe would bring them right back to reality by saying, "Just the facts, sir."

In our work, as we seek the one great idea that will deliver measurable results, the ideal strategy is to emulate Joe Friday. Before we present any idea or solution for our advertising, we need to gather the facts. Just the facts.

This prevents our personal likes and dislikes from muddying the waters. We want the facts, just the facts and only the facts please.

Below are the questions I ask to gather the facts. It is an actual interview, with some fictional exaggerations, in a real case of a real client in Tennessee. The names have been changed to protect the innocent. You will see what I mean by specific answers as we interview "Big Bob" owner of Fireworks Heaven.

Q: Briefly, what is the history of your business?

Big Bob: I first opened in 1989 as Fireworks City. We had a little problem so I moved the business.

Q: What was the little problem?

Big Bob: There was an electrical short. It started a small fire, but then the whole place exploded back in 2002. We got a lot of bad press so I changed the name when we moved here and re-opened as Fireworks Heaven in 2003.

Q: What is the trend in sales today?

Big Bob: Sales are OK but I'm getting nervous. I should be doing more. The bank is on my back for loan payments, and my wife left me and she wants child support and I tell you my drinking problem is behind me, but those AA meetings get old and then…

Q: (Interrupting) Just the facts, sir! I need real numbers. I want the percentages and the dollar amounts. I can't solve this marketing challenge without the facts.

Big Bob: Well I wanted to do $800,000 in sales last year, but we only did $700,000. In the old location, I almost hit $1 million and I was big, real big. Is that what you mean by the facts?

Q: Yes sir, it is. Keep coming with the numbers and the percentages. Let's try another question. What are you selling here?

Big Bob: Things that go bang, ka-blewie and make nice lights in the night. Wow, can I make the night come alive and you know…

Q: (Smacking Big Bob on the head with a notepad) I'm going to ask you again to give me only the facts. Do I have to slap you again or are you ready to talk?

Big Bob: No, no, please, I don't want to go bankrupt. I'll give you the facts.

Q: Let's try again. What do you sell? Be specific. What are the big sellers? Give me the facts, sir, just the facts. What are your products or services by volume and profit? Give me some figures or percentages.

Big Bob: Well, by volume: air burst rockets, 50 percent; cherry bombs, etc., 35 percent; twirlers and sparklers, 15 percent. By profit: air burst rockets, 45 percent markup. The rest is 20 percent markup.

Q: That's what I want, sir: the facts. You're doing fine. Now, who are the core customers? I mean, the people you see the most often, not the unusual customers, but your everyday, steady bread and butter?

Big Bob: That's easy. It is almost all male. Ages 16 to 39. 70 percent blue collar, NASCAR fans. Adrenaline freaks. 90 percent Caucasian. From a 100 mile radius. Is that what you want when you say only specific facts like percentages?

Q: Yes sir, just the facts. You are doing just fine. Now, what is your seasonality? Be specific if you want your ads to work!

Big Bob: 65 percent of our business is July 4th. 35 percent is the New Year. The rest of the time I might as well close down and go to Vegas, but the guys at Gambling Anonymous say I can't.

Q: Who is the competition and how do you compare?

Big Bob: Fireworks Frannie drives me crazy. She has half my selection but I'm in a bad location. My prices are 20 percent cheaper, and she still sells more than I do.

Q: Where and when do you advertise? Please name each media you use. What do you get in terms of spots or space? How well does each work and what does each cost? Let's do them one at a time.

Q: Print advertising?

Big Bob: Full-page sports section on July 2nd and December 26th. I'm not sure it works as well as it once did. It's $3,000 each time.

Q: Radio advertising?

Big Bob: A full week prior to each holiday on nine stations. I run with the Conglomerate Group, about 20 spots each station. I run for three weeks prior July 4th and to New Years. I think it's about $10,000 each.

Q: Cable TV?

Big Bob: Two systems in July and December. Each one gives me 100 spots to run. We spread it out over 10 different channels: $4,000 for July and $4,000 for December.

Q: Broadcast TV?

Big Bob: Late-night shows and overnights on WBAG and also on WCOW, not sure it works. I think I get a lot of spots that run overnight mostly. They charge me about $500 on each station when I run on the week before the holiday.

Q: Direct mail?

Big Bob: No direct mail. I tried it, but got a lot of it back with bad addresses. It cost me $7,000. My customer base seems to move a lot.

Q: What about billboards, Yellow Pages, or anything else?

Big Bob: I cut out yellow pages years ago. I have one board on the highway. It is $500 a month and it is great. I get people here because it has directions. I'm planning to try movie theater ads this year.

Q: Of all the advertising in all those different media, in which do you have the most faith as far as measurable results and as money well spent? What really works for you?

Big Bob: Well, the billboard for sure, and then maybe the radio, but after that I'm not sure about anything else.

Q: What about your web site?

Big Bob: I don't have one.

Q: Gasp! Do you know that is like being in business with no phone?

Big Bob: Okay, I'll get a web site.

Q: Describe your usual message. How do you deal with price? Do you have any consistent theme or slogan?

Big Bob: I always show the newest big bang rockets. That's what people want. I never mention prices and our slogan is "Big Bob has Big Bangs for Big Boys."

Q: Let's look at your first-time customer. When a new customer finds you for the very first time, what do they usually ask you or what do they usually want?

Big Bob: A lot of them are just discovering us again. They think we closed down after the fire so they are surprised to find us open again. Some of them get nervous when they see the hideous burn scars on my face. Should I wear a mask? Do the scars bother you?

Q: I would see a plastic surgeon if I were you sir or audition for a role in Phantom of the Opera, but that has nothing to do with the facts. I have one last question for you. I call it my Magic Wand question. If you could accomplish any one thing with your advertising, what do you want to accomplish? And please don't tell me more customers. That's obvious. I want something more specific.

Big Bob: That's easy. I want more people to know we are back in business; that we have rebuilt the store after the explosion and it's bigger and better than ever. And we are a lot cheaper than Fireworks Frannie and I would like to reach more middle- and upper-class families to buy the more expensive fireworks.

Q: Sir only one wish, remember. Which is it? The location issue, the price issue or the wish for more middle class families?

Big Bob: The location. I need to make my new location clear, so all my old customers can find me.

What you just read was detective work. It was somewhat tedious; maybe even a bit boring for you as the reader. In real life it takes about 20 to 30 minutes to sit down and go through these basic questions. The good advertising sales reps will do it with their clients and business owners can do it themselves with their employees to gather the facts. But in any case, the fact gathering should occur before any money is spent or any copy is written. I literally ask each and every one of these questions every time I try to help improve someone's advertising.

The mantra to justify all these questions is simple. Prescription without diagnosis is malpractice.

The most important question of the lot is "The Magic Wand" question.

Here is how it works. Pretend you wave the Magic Wand and are granted one wish in your advertising. But there is a hook. Not only do you get just one wish, but that one wish must be specific and realistic.

For example, wishing for more sales or more traffic or more market share is way too general and is not in the least bit specific.

Wishing to double sales overnight is not realistic.

But when Big Bob wished he could make his new location well known, that was a specific and realistic wish.

Therefore, we wrote a campaign focused on making his new location very clear. The entire ad was devoted to that singular copy point. We focused on his Magic Wand wish.

It was indeed the primary issue which helped to bring back most of his old customers. Wish granted!

RULE THREE:

K.I.S.S.

Let's examine another real-life ad that failed to produce results. The owner of a Michigan heating business, just south of the Arctic Circle, wanted to sell a new type of geothermal furnace to cut energy costs. Hence, his Magic Wand Wish was "to sell geothermal furnaces." The detective work was excellent. The goal was identified and clear. The ad he produced did focus on geothermal furnaces and stayed focused on nothing but the concept of geothermal heating. So why did it fail? It failed, because the message was too complex.

Let's see if you can guess why. Do your own test. Find a reasonably intelligent person and read this script to them fast. Remember, it's just a 30-second time slot.

Announcer:

Fuel prices are up.

Is another energy crisis coming?

Are you tired of those high oil bills?

Well, there is a way to cut those bills in half.

Let the Thermal Furnace and Energy Company come to your home, install a new geothermal furnace and cut your high energy bill in half by using ground energy to heat your home this winter.

Here is how it works:

A high-capacity, heat-absorbing solution circulates through pipes in a loop in the ground underneath your home.

There it is heated by ambient ground temperatures and the absorbed heat is carried to your house through a series of pipes.

Inside, another high-capacity BTU thermal heater pressurizes the solution, raises its temperature and then distributes the adiabatically enhanced heat evenly to all levels of your home.

For more details, contact the Thermal Furnace and Energy Company in Traverse City.

Thermal Furnace: Serving Your Energy Needs in Traverse City

Phone them now at 413-255-6756. That's 413-255-6756!

When I do seminars and play this ad for the audience I am usually greeted with howling laughter, as one by one, they give up trying to follow the ad to some rational conclusion.

The only exception is the occasional scientist or engineer in the group. I then ask him or her to explain the concept of a geothermal furnace and how it works. Even then, the audience has a difficult time understanding the complex operation of a technical piece of equipment. You can see the dilemma from an advertising standpoint. How do you deal with complex concepts or technical equipment in a short period of time?

If it takes an Einstein to understand the message, we have a problem. $E = mc$ squared works for rocket scientists but it just confuses most of our audiences.

Keep it simple, stupid!

How simple, you ask? I design my ads for an audience that I assume is either half-listening or half-watching most commercials. I pretend they are all third graders.

If you think I underestimate the concentration level of the average target audience, you're wrong. The problem isn't their intelligence or their education, it's simply listeners and viewers usually don't pay full attention to advertising (Super Bowl ads excepted). They're driving cars, reading magazines, talking on cell phones, making breakfast, surfing the net or eating dinner. This imposes severe limitations on our ability to get their attention, much less deliver anything more than the simplest of messages.

In the Thermal Furnace and Energy Company ad, information was presented in an unnecessarily complicated format as seen from the advertiser's point of view. The ad attempted to explain how the furnace actually works rather than focus on the benefits it provided to the customer.

So let's rewrite it. To do so, we assume the audience has a low attention span, and we want to emphasize the major point that the customer needs to know: What's the benefit for me? How does this sound?

Announcer:

Tired of high oil bills?

Sick of the oil barons gouging you?

Doesn't it make you mad?

Well, there is a way to cut your bills in half. Go to www.geothermal.com.

Yes cut your oil bill in half.

Homeowners, it's time to get mad and fight the greedy pigs.

Cut your monthly bill in half with a new geothermal furnace. Go to geothermal.com.

Or just call us.

That's right. Cut your bill in half with a geothermal furnace.

It's easy to make the change and we do all the work for you.

And it will cut your bill in half.

To find out how to cut your energy bill in half visit our web site or call us.

Thermal Furnace and Energy Company in Traverse City at www.geothermal.com.

Note the changes? We cut the unnecessary technical language, used simpler terms and concentrated on the main benefit for the homeowner: "Cut your bill in half."

And did you notice how many times we used the word "you" or "your" when speaking directly to the customer? And most importantly in the web era, we pushed a web address that is easy to remember.

Of course, it's easier said than done. I know that focusing on one idea or one copy point is very difficult. Very often an ad starts out focused and ends up with clutter. Usually the advertiser tells me, "But I just have to let people know about our history, location, heritage, knowledge, and expertise.

My reply is simple. The fewer points in the ad the greater the chance for success. The more points you add, the greater the chance of failure. So what is the ideal number of points that ensures success? Simply One...... Uno! Ein! Ichi!

Let's look at the data.

By my calculations and research, in America today the average failure rate for local companies that advertise in major media is approximately 65 percent.

The average number of copy points in those ads is seven. When the number of copy points is reduced to one, the failure drops to about 40 percent. As I will show you in later chapters, even that can be improved upon, so read on if you want to see how to get your failure rate down to 20 percent! Don't forget you can always drive traffic to your web site, where more complex details and information can be better explained.

Let's look at another example I encountered during my travels. A lawyer, a Miss Bee Brown, in Macon, Georgia, had asked for help on a commercial for her law firm. (Why in the south does "Miss" mean she is most likely married, frumpy and over 40 years old?) She was one smart lady but, bless her heart, her ads were really awful. (Why in the south do the words "bless her heart" always lead to some serious criticism?) In the ad she listed all the different types of cases she could handle: divorce proceedings, personal injury, workman's compensation, medical malpractice, drunken driving and estate planning (6 copy points). Then she talked up her 35 years of experience (7).

She mentioned she was a member of the Georgia Bar Association (8) and she offered free consultations (9).

After copious detective work I learned that her "Magic Wand Wish" was to attract clients who had social security compensation problems.

"Miss Bee," I said, "reducing copy points increases an ad's success rate. Therefore, I think you should concentrate on only social security claims; the area you prefer and an area with excellent profit potential."

She nodded her head in approval. I continued, "Using social security claims as your primary focus, you also need to let your customers know what's in it for them.

I like to quote FedEx as a great example. FedEx doesn't talk about their 400 airplanes, 10,000 employees or their horde of delivery trucks. Instead, they talk about what they offer to the customer, which is to absolutely, positively, guaranteed overnight delivery."

I asked her to similarly focus on what her clients want, perhaps a message, such as "I'll get you the monthly social security check you deserve."

Failure to follow rule three can especially doom any ad. It is just that simple.

RULE FOUR:

K.I.S.S. WITH CONSISTENCY

As an advertiser, local ad agency or a local advertising salesperson, sooner or later you get the killer ad on the air, of course remembering that greatness is defined as something that produces measurable results.

I'm often asked, "How long should a good ad run?"

When good advertisers retire the killer ad it's usually for one simple reason; it no longer produces results. No results mean it's no longer a killer ad.

Madison Avenue agencies will run a killer ad forever. They do surveys, focus groups and measurements to rate the performance of an ad campaign. Bottom line, if the ad works, the ad keeps airing. It's kind of like a racehorse that keeps running races, providing it continues to generate winnings.

The Pillsbury Doughboy is still producing today, but the moment the cute, little, pudgy guy stops ringing the cash register, he'll be fried dough.

Local advertisers, by contrast, often kill great ads sooner than they should. Time and time again I encounter advertisers who discover a successful message then abandon it prematurely. Usually, their rationale lies along the lines that they feel the ad was getting tired, stale, and it was time to freshen up the campaign.

Translation:

"I don't care if the ad is still working, my friends are bored with it, my family is sick of it, and frankly I'm tired of it too."

Rather than reinvent the wheel I want you to stay with a winning message ad infinitum. If you have found a winning idea, stay with it! You can still change some part of your message, but never change the basics.

One of the best ways to maintain consistency is to select a positioning statement that you want to stay with for the long run. By positioning statement I mean a simple phrase or theme that details or draws attention to your product. It instantly defines who you are in the crowded marketplace. For example, the photo at the beginning of this chapter represents my positioning as the "Guru of Ads."

Most national advertisers have some form of positioning statement or theme which instantly focuses you on their product.

The GEICO gecko: "Give us 15 minutes to save 15 percent on your auto insurance."
Foster's Beer: "Australian for beer."
Allstate: "You're in good hands."

The national advertisers are usually pretty good about using themes that are not only consistent but also quickly identifiable. Local advertisers should apply the same strategy to their positioning statements.

Let me clarify:

Right now, I'm writing this on a Southwest Airlines flight 35,000 feet above Nebraska. Do you know their theme? Hint: It's all about freedom.

Give up? It's "The symbol of freedom." In their ads, you always hear that little "ding" and the words, "You are now free to move about the country." I suppose they're saying that Southwest provides us more flexible, easier and cheaper opportunities to get around.

Seeing as I'm trapped in seat 17F, I'm going to grab an in-flight magazine and look at some of the local ads. I'm looking for positioning statements or themes to see if they make sense. Here are three examples and what I think of them.

1) Here's one for a law firm: "When you need help, we are here for you."

My reaction: Weak! They're here for me? What does that mean? I wonder if I can get free help or maybe just a babysitter when I need one.

2) This next one is an ad promoting a shopping mall: "Shopping that revolves around you."

My reaction: Confusion! There must be a merry-go-round in the food court.

3) Another for a big city hospital: "Your heart is our passion."

My reaction: Terror. My god, are they cannibals?

It strikes me that the positioning statements in these examples are pretty useless. They're easy to read, but just plain hard to understand, not to mention vague.

However, I do see two examples of good ads which illustrate how to make a positioning statement simple and easy to understand.

1) A seminar hosted by Donald Trump: "Experts Teach You How to Get Rich."

My reaction: Mmmmm, rich sounds good.

2) An airport parking lot in Las Vegas: "We have sheltered airport parking."

My reaction: Right on. That means my car might not be an oven when I return home.

Now let's be more specific about positioning statements. Remember, by positioning statement I mean a simple phrase or theme that details or draws attention to your product. It instantly defines who you are in the crowded marketplace.

Right now I will give you my brief explanation of a positioning statement. If you want the detailed version, I suggest you read <u>Positioning the Battle for your Mind</u> by Reis and Trout. I only will recommend two books in my book and that's one of them.

The Guru's definition of positioning:

In your brain, my brain, and the brains of the people we want to reach with advertising, there are a bunch of little compartments. Each compartment has a name like "Lost

Loves of My Life" or "My Darkest Secrets" or "Baseball Teams" or "Best Friends" or "Fast Food Places" or "German Beer." We each have many of these compartments in our brains.

But compartments by themselves are small, like tiny little mailboxes in a giant post office. Let me show you what I mean by examining a compartment that is surely in your brain. I'll call it "Breakfast Cereals."

In the space below, write the names of as many breakfast cereals as you can.

1)   7)

2)   8)

3)   9)

4)   10)

5)   11)

6)   12)

I'll bet you wrote down around seven or eight cereals before you started struggling. Your brain's breakfast cereal compartment just cannot go deeper because seven is the average number of categories people can remember.

Now imagine you are standing in the breakfast cereal aisle at the local mega grocery store. There must be 100 different brands stocked in the cereal aisle! In fact, there are undoubtedly documented cases of moms gone missing in action searching for that special cereal their five year old is demanding. There are that many choices.

In advertising, the winning cereals are the ones you were able to remember and write down in the little exercise above. Those names are "positioned" in your brain as the more likely candidates for purchase. The name that you wrote down first is the ultimate winner; positioned as number one in your mind. The same applies to the multitude of other compartments.

McDonald's almost always wins in the fast food category. Coke or Pepsi wins for colas. Budweiser wins for beer. Your ex wins for spouses from hell. Paris wins under the romantic-city category. For me, Firestone Double Barrel Ale wins under best micro beer.

On your local level, the positioning battle is no different. Someone surely claims the best local restaurant or the best grocery store or the best pizza category in your hometown.

You can quickly see that ideally your advertising will have that slogan or theme which puts your product at the top of a particular category.

Now what about those of you who do not already own a position of your own? Claim one. But, unless you have lots of loose cash to blow, don't go after the one already staked out and guarded by a well established competitor. Look for a smaller niche or a variant you can claim as your own. Sometimes this leads to a progression of ever smaller niches as more competitors use the same technique. Here is my absolute favorite example of such a progression. I literally saw these three billboards one after another in Memphis, Tennessee.

First billboard: Montgomery & Montgomery Specialists in Personal Injury Cases
Second billboard: Clampmore, Briggs and Bellmeade for the Serious Personal Injury
Third billboard: Call John Drake if Your Family has Suffered a Death Injury

We started this lesson by discussing the need for consistency in your advertising. As long as you are getting results, I want you to stay with a consistent look and message. Again, positioning is the phrase or words you use and stick with to identify your niche in the marketplace.

Let's finish this lesson with one more example of another local lawyer who succeeded by claiming a very small niche in his advertising over the years.

His statement was this: "If you get arrested tonight call DUI-MIKE."

I love working with lawyers because they are usually pretty smart and I especially admire the ones who have gone into practice on their own. They're hungry and aggressive, as opposed to the fat cats in the huge firms atop the Hilton who sneer at advertising.

This particular individual was, above all, consistent. He always appeared personally in his ads. His message always focused on drunken driving litigation. He unceasingly pledged his best efforts towards combating drunken driving charges. Most importantly, he always advertised his phone number. Not only was he consistent in his message, but he always advertised heavily through the same media.

I'm normally not a fan of print advertising, but in this case, I think he was a genius. He purchased the advertising space above the urinals in bars all across town. Anyone out swilling beer who made multiple trips to the john couldn't help but notice his message.

He also supplemented his advertising with radio and TV ads, which aired after midnight. So again, anyone arrested on their late drive home immediately thought of DUI-MIKE.

His positioning in the market was equally simple and consistent. He claimed to be a drunken driving litigation specialist. He repeated it so often that in time, he automatically came to mind for those crazy drivers who were drinking and driving.

Rule Four: KISS consistently. If your ad is producing results and you have a positioning statement that is unique to your product, stay with it.

RULE FIVE:

KILL THE CLICHÉS (BEFORE THEY KILL YOU)

Have you ever wondered why so many advertisers repeat the same tired phrases and clichés over and over? It is as if they are all parrots. It is as if they have no original language of their own. They just repeat words we have heard a thousand times. Brawwwwk! Polly wants a cracker!

I'm now ready to take you on an up-close look at one of the most depraved, desolate and desperate advertising destinations on planet Earth, the deadly Zone of Clichés. I like to call it the ZOC.

How much do I despise the ZOC? I live near Boston, so culturally I'm obliged to hate the New York Yankees. But even though I believe the Yankees are the true embodiment of the evil empire, I hate them far less than I hate ZOC!

Here's why. The Yankees can (and often do) crush my spirit but they can't hurt my business. The ZOC is another story. It can cause sales to plummet and customers to desert you. It can also allow your competition to eat you alive.

How? Let me describe the Zone of Clichés in more detail so you can understand what it is and more importantly, how to avoid it.

The Zone of Clichés is an omnipresent electronic disease, the tentacles of which reach every man, woman and child in America. It is characterized by advertising messages loaded with worn-out words, phrases and pictures that are nothing but clichés. When you include clichés, especially old ones, to your advertising, you generate ZOC. The effect on viewers or listeners is an instant stupor, generating nothing but lethargy and ambivalence, not to mention immediate channel surfing.

Look at the following list. Recognize the clichés? Feel the ZOC?

Quality service
Friendly, professional staff
Locally owned and operated
In business for 30 years
Serving your needs
We care about you
From our family to yours
Conveniently located
You can trust us

Now use them in a commercial and you instantly enter the dreaded ZOC. Experience for yourself its effects. Here's an example from a 60-second radio ad for our dear friend Edna and her flower shop in Eugene, Oregon.

Announcer:

This Mother's Day, shop at Edna's Flower Shop. Along with a fine selection of flowers and gifts, you will be treated to quality service guaranteed by a friendly, professional staff.

Locally owned and operated, Edna's Flower Shop has been in business for over 30 years, serving all your floral needs. Satisfaction guaranteed, because we care about you and your special mother. There are hundreds of items to choose from our gift shop. From our family to yours, we wish all moms a happy Mother's Day.

We are conveniently located just off Main Street across from the mall. Be sure to mention this ad to get a special discount on all our roses. We deliver and we are open until 7:00 PM weekdays and then until 4:00 PM on Saturdays. We are closed Monday. Call us at 207-566-7867 or visit our web site at ednasflowershop.com.

And remember, when flowers come from Edna's they come with our exclusive promise of satisfaction. We also carry an unforgettable line of cards and mementos for Mom. Flowers, gifts and so much more, it's all yours at Edna's Flower Shop.

Argggggh. Please save us all from the diatribe of clichés.
Edna just used 60 seconds to turn your brain into mush,
assuming you would have actually listened to the whole
thing.

The average listener, if he or she heard anything, would
have heard this:

Announcer:
This Mother's Day choose Edna's Flower shop. Blah blah
blah blah blah blah blah blah blah blah blah. Blah blah
blah blah blah blah, Edna's Flower Shop. Blah blah blah
blah blah blah blah blah. You will get the blah blah blah
for Mother's Day blah blah blah blah blah blah blah blah
blah blah. Blah blah blah blah blah blah blah blah. We
wish all moms a happy Mother's Day. Gift shop, Blah blah
blah blah blah blah. Just off the main street across from the
mall. Be sure to mention this ad to get a special discount
on all our roses. Blah blah blah blah blah blah blah blah
blah blah blah blah blah blah blah blah blah blah blah.
Blah blah blah blah. Edna's Flower Shop dot com. Blah
blah blah! Greeting cards and mementos, blah, blah blah,
blah, blah, blah blah blah. Flowers gifts and blah blah blah
blah blah blah blah!

That is, he or she wouldn't have heard anything. The end result is no result.

Effective advertising begins by purging clichés from your advertising. Let's call upon the teachings of a somewhat older prophet, who wrote mostly about radio advertising, yet whose teachings still apply to all media. His name is Roy Williams.

In his book, <u>The Wizard of Ads</u>, (my second and last book recommendation), he specifically draws attention to the actual words used in commercials. His mantra: "Change the wording." That is, look at the words in an ad, resist using clichés and instead, use synonyms.

Let's go back to the previous example and take just a few of the clichés and try to reword them, avoiding the clichés. So for Edna's Flower Shop, we change some words:

"Quality service" becomes "You will be treated like a rock star."

"30 years in business" becomes "Grandpa started us off back when the Beatles were popular."

"Conveniently located" becomes "You don't need a GPS to find us."

I'm not claiming that any of those copy points are valuable, but I am saying that by changing the words you might at least be heard because you eliminated the clichés.

Avoiding the ZOC helps, but I've discovered that there's another step in this process which goes beyond changing only the wording of an ad. As Roy Williams advocates, you can make your point better if you change the words as we did above. The next step requires you to add specific proof of the claims you are making. Pretend you are the customer and use the "What's in it for me" test. See how it reads now, having purged the clichés and added specific proof of what is in it for the customer.

"Quality service" became "you will be treated like a rock star."
The next step is to add in the explanation of what that means to the customer.
"You will be treated like a rock star, as we offer champagne to all our shoppers."

"30 years in business" became "Grandpa started us off back when the Beatles were popular."

Now we move to what it means to the customer.

"Grandpa started us off back when the Beatles were popular and he has kept our prices almost as low as they were then."

"Conveniently located" became "you don't need a GPS to find us."

And we add in what it means to the customer;

"You won't need a GPS to find us. We are right smack downtown, so you can get in and out during a coffee break."

So far, we have dealt with just the spoken copy as you might hear it in a radio ad. The same points apply to the spoken copy in television advertising, but now we must expose the visual clichés that create the television version of the ZOC. Let's take a look at some common visual clichés. Surely you've seen them:

- the auto dealer, walking down a row of cars
- the lawyer at his desk with a cabinet of books behind him
- the furniture ad with the long camera shot, showing a showroom full of furniture
- the customer shaking hands with the business owner

- the glittering diamond revolving on a pedestal of light

Visual clichés and the images themselves also create the ZOC. Viewers now see nothing but the same old blah blah blah.

And if you really want to create the perfect ZOC, run an ad that uses both verbal and visual clichés. In Edna's example, we could use a visual sweeping camera shot of the store then show some flowers and gifts bought by a happy customer shaking hands with Edna. The grand finale would show mom getting her flowers delivered to her bed by her adorable, little kids.

By now you should not only understand the Zone of Clichés and its devastating effects on advertising but you most likely can confess to having run cliché-ridden ads in the past or (gasp) it's in your advertising right now. Go ahead, admit it. Cleanse yourself of the memories, as only then can we move on to the healing process.

Remember one mission of this book is to turn ourselves from sheep (Baaaaaaa) to advertising lions. Confession helps us all heal and move on.

Let's do a little exercise together to exorcise those visual clichés. Change the cliché-ridden visualizations to something different. Then add a qualifying statement to address what's in it for the customer—just as we did with the radio examples.

Here are some real-life changes from real-life ads, which worked very well.

The auto dealer walking down a row of cars becomes a midget who talks about his tiny prices.

The lawyer at his desk with a cabinet of books behind him becomes a lawyer surrounded by his staff carrying baseball bats promising to beat the hell out of the insurance companies to get you a fat check.

The long camera shot showing a showroom full of furniture becomes a television quiz show in which the host asks the contestants, "How many couches are on the floor right now at Joe's Furniture?" The host clarifies that having 1,000 couches means you get the color, style and price you want.

One last suggestion: Don't trust yourself. You may be too close to your own business with a tendency to talk about yourself and forget to explain what's in it for the customer. I confess. I did it to myself when writing this book. My original title was going to be <u>Kick A$$ Advertising</u> with the subtitle <u>The Rules of the Guru</u>. After being smacked upside the head by a fellow consultant, I changed the title to <u>The Guru's Rules for Local Advertising</u> to make it clear the theme was local ads. Local advertising is what you, the reader, are interested in. The subtitle became <u>It's All About Measurable Results</u>, which tells you, the customer, exactly why you should buy it!

RULE SIX:

K.I.S.S. WITH STRENGTH

I am a lion.

(Grrr)

I will persist until I succeed

I was not born into this world in defeat

Nor does failure course in my veins

I am not a sheep

(Baaaaa)

Waiting to be prodded by my shepherd

No! I am a lion.

(Grrrrrrrrrrr!)

I refuse total, to walk, to sleep or to eat with the sheep

(Baaaaaaaaaaaaaa!)
For their destiny is the slaughterhouse of failure
I am a lion
(Grrrrrrrrrrrrrrrrrrrrrrr!!!)
I will persist until I succeed

The preceding is an excerpt taken from a book on sales by Og Mandino. I have modified it a little, especially by adding the sound effects. It is a mantra I have chanted to myself a thousand times over the past years to help stay motivated. I put it in this chapter as both an attention getter and acknowledge the strength of attitude. I suggest you read it aloud with great emphasis on the sound effects when you need to improve your attitude.

Now let's get on with the explanation of what I mean by kissing with strength.

In this chapter we'll discuss the need to focus your advertising on the one true strength of your business, plus your personal one true strength.

Notice I said the one true strength of *your business* plus *your personal* one true strength.

First, it's worth a quick review of the Keep It Simple mantra that we discussed in Rule 3. Remember, the goal there was to get you focused on one singular copy point.

So why am I now injecting all this stuff about *your business* and *your personal* strength on top of the chapter on simplicity? Here is why. The overall process of simplifying copy points sounds easy, but in reality it is very difficult. I'm asking you to not only narrow your ad to a single copy point, but also to make sure it represents *your* one true business strength plus *your* one true personal strength.

First let us discuss the concept of your one true business strength. We will do the personal strength assessment later.

As a Guru who has interviewed thousands of people, the process of filtering a large list of copy points down to the important ones has become relatively easy for me. With a little research a business' strengths are usually readily apparent.

Alas, for advertisers, local station sales reps and even local ad agencies, achieving simplicity is elusive. The difficulty almost always originates from those individuals closest to the business. If we are to point the gnarly finger of blame at those responsible for cluttering up ads with too many copy points, the fault falls first and foremost on the advertiser. Blame falls next on friends and family of the advertiser and finally on the advertising sales rep or advertising agencies that, quite naturally, go along with anything the client wants in order to get an order.

The least blame, surprisingly, lies with the writers and producers of the actual commercials. They're usually just taking instructions from the culprits above, and even though they won't say so, they hate the long laundry list of copy points. The solution is simple—focus on the one true business strength.

The key is to look for that single issue or strength you wish to highlight, and then make it the focus of your commercials. Sometimes it is as easy as identifying the elephant knocking on your front door. But often we feel that there are multiple choices. How do we find that one strength upon which to focus our message?

Usually it falls into one of the following categories:

Volume

Profit

Growth Opportunity

Seasonality

Let's take a look at each of these as they apply to any one business.

Volume. Imagine that you're a Ford Dealer in Wyoming. Maybe you're stuck with too much inventory and you want to run an ad campaign to move cars quickly. But a look at your track record over the past few years suggests that car sales are your weakness. In fact, your sales, according to sheer numbers, have traditionally been 70 percent trucks and SUVs. In that case, advertising cars is insane. Your strength is trucks and SUVs.

Profit. A great way to get focused on strength is to consider the product or service that generates the highest profit in a business. Consider this hypothetical eye doctor. Eighty percent of patient volume is in eye exams and normal prescriptions. Only 20 percent is in Lasik surgeries. But sweet mother of pearl, the profit on a prescription is $20 and the profit on a Lasik procedure is $1,200. This makes a solid argument that the eye doctor's strength is in Lasik business and not eye exams.

Growth Opportunity. I learned this lesson in Miami. I was making sales calls in one of the city's trendy beach sections. I met with a restaurant owner who was looking for advice. When I asked about his strengths, he quickly pointed out that his core customer base was "old, filthy rich, on walkers, in wheelchairs, with portable oxygen tanks and about to die." If I had followed my standard rule and identified that older core customer group as his strength, I would have guaranteed that his business would literally have died off with them. In this case, the need for a new customer base was clear, crystal clear, and the ad campaign we agreed upon was geared to the growth opportunity of attracting 60 year old diners instead of the current 80 year olds who were dying off at his lunch tables. Under future opportunity for almost everyone reading this book there is surely something in the exploding world of the internet.

Seasonality. Over the years I have learned that you usually can't fight the seasonality of any business. If sales are exceptionally strong in spring, then use your ad money in spring. Using a fish analogy (I never fish), "Fish when fish are biting." In Tucson, Arizona, I worked with a small chocolate shop with a small ad budget. The shop took my advice and spent its entire annual budget on one day, the day before Valentine's Day! The campaign was a fantastic success.

After you identify the one strength to promote, there is one more variable to consider. Another critical question remains to be answered; where should you invest your advertising dollars? The important point is that advertising budgets must be invested in just a very few select media outlets. By concentrating your ad budget into just a few media outlets it will air with strength. Spread it all over creation and it becomes a weakling.

This has been one of the most dramatic changes in advertising that has occurred over the last 20 years. Allow me a short historical review. Once upon a time, the concept called "Media Mix" dictated how ad budgets were spent. To wit, the budget was spread throughout a mix of media. TV, radio, newspaper, magazines, billboards, etc. were all used to get the message out. It was a good strategy then because there were only three TV networks and maybe five good radio stations, and newspapers still had large circulation.

That day is over and the fragmentation of the telecommunications industry is such that media mix no longer works. Not surprisingly, newspapers are definitely not the outlet of choice, if you want to reach anyone under 50. The exceptions being those free weekly shoppers and local weekly community papers.

What works now is a concentration of effort in electronic media. My partner, Jim Doyle, was one of the visionaries who saw this trend coming years ago.

Here is how he explains it. Imagine that your ad budget is contained in a pitcher of water, and you spend it by filling several glasses, representing your individual media choices. In the old day of "media mix," you would pour a little bit of your budget into the newspaper glass, a little into the country radio station glass, a little bit more in the rock radio station glass, etc. However, over the years, the number of TV, radio stations and cable channels have increased so dramatically that the "little bits" are lost in the clutter.

As Jim Doyle advises, "Instead of a little bit here and a little bit there, pick media outlets you can dominate and fill those glasses until they are overflowing. At that point, you get the most efficient results for your money." Forget the shotgun approach. Now you want to dominate fewer outlets by advertising frequently enough to break through the clutter. It should go without saying, "If you can't dominate, don't waste the money!"

But what's a good definition of strong frequency? Here's my general guideline for a given week, assuming you use a 6am to midnight schedule.

* Radio - Run 40 spots on one radio station.

* Cable TV - Run 40 spots per week per channel for any given cable channel like HGTV.

* TV - For a broadcast TV station, forget that 6am to midnight schedule or the run of station schedule most of us call ROS for short. Now the game changes and it is all about domination of a specific program. So you want at least three spots per week per program. For example, if you're running in the morning news, you want to be there at least three times a week. Five a week works even better.

Of course, there are many variations to these guidelines, but sheer domination seems to work the best. You can choose to dominate one day a week, just overnights, or maybe only one day a year. If you can't dominate something, do nothing.

A beautiful example of domination used in a campaign ran on WFNX, an FM station in New England, which sold all of its advertising slots from May 25 to July 4 to the drink company Snapple. During that small time frame, WFNX listeners heard nothing but Snapple, Snapple, and more Snapple commercials. No car dealers, no beer ads, no furniture stores, just Snapple. WFNX commanded a small percent of the New England audience, but Snapple commanded 100 percent of the attention of anyone who listened to that station.

Now for the same amount of money, I'm guessing the Snapple folks could have bought one lousy Super Bowl spot. Sure it would have reached a lot more people than WFNX. But if given the choice I would make the exact same decision to dominate WFNX!

In your marketing, if faced with the choice of buying one spot in the high school championship game, the big college game or the last episode of a killer TV show, I hope you will apply the same logic. One wretched commercial will do nothing. If you can't dominate, don't do it.

Okay, that concludes our discussion of your business strength. We even threw in that section on how to air your message with the strength of high frequency.

Let's now talk about your personal strength to make sure it matches up with what you must have in your business strength. After all, if the strength of your business is based on legal talent and you have none, then you have a problem. No match! In fact I now go one step further and contend that it is an unfixable problem.

What did you say? Unfixable? Many of you will object and cry out that lack of legal talent in my example can be overcome. You have seen the motivational speakers at your annual conventions. You have watched Oprah and Dr. Phil say to us over and over, "You can be anything you want to be!" Now here comes The Guru saying, no nay never, no nay never no more! In fact, The Guru says that, "In business you can try anything you wanna try, but if it's not your inherent talent the business is gonna die."

On the other hand, take a woman running a tax accounting firm. She tells me the strength of her business in both volume and profit is corporate tax returns. She is also talented at bean counting; a talent for numbers is her personal strength. Match made!

So what is your one true personal strength or talent or ability? Write it down right here. It is _____

Hopefully you have already identified your one true business strength from the paragraphs above. Write it down right here. It is _____

Do we have a match?

RULE SEVEN:

IDENTIFY THE POINT OF ENTRY

Seven rules down, seven to go!

We now honor an event which always starts at 7am on the 7th day of the 7th month of every year. It is the running of the bulls in Pamplona, Spain.

What you see above are bulls entering the stadium gate leading to the bull ring. Why are they charging straight past this gate with no worries? Hey, it is a bull ring. Bulls die there. Well, they are not worried because at this point of entry there is only one thing on their minds. They are just a couple of bulls following a bunch of cows. Mmmmm cows.

But we are advertising to humans. So let us move from Pamplona to your business. The point of entry for your business is the one thing that induces a new, repeat, a new customer to make that actual first step to contact you. It's best explained with this real-life example:

Pretend for a second that you're returning home to your spouse and kiddies and you live in a god-forsaken, flat, arid desert surrounded by oil rigs and other fragile humans. West Texas comes to mind and you're right, it's not one of my favorite areas in which to work, especially in the summer.

Imagine it is August with a heat wave pushing temperatures close to 110 degrees. A dry west wind is filtering hot dust into homes, threatening to choke the goldfish. You arrive home to discover the air conditioning has failed and your family is developing the first stages of heat prostration. Your obvious concern is to cool your house. You need an air-conditioning company and someone who can fix your A/C, and fix it fast.

You are at what we call the point of entry or POE. You don't give a damn about the history of the company, their credentials or even who owns the business. You just want your air conditioning fixed quickly.

Now let's change roles and pretend you're in charge of advertising for an air-conditioning company in the area. In the old days, you might have relied only on the Yellow Pages. But alas, today life moves too fast. You want to get inside the brain of that homeowner before the system breaks. You want your name to be on his or her mind even before your services are needed.

So your ad is drop-dead simple. The point of entry is a broken air-conditioning system and that's all you need to address in your ads. In short, you should brainwash potential customers like this:

- Broken air conditioner? Call Help-333 or go to FastFreds.com and we'll be there fast and fix it fast.

- Call Help-333 or go to FastFreds.com for an immediate fix on broken air conditioning.

- Fast Fred specializes in immediate service to cool you off fast. Call Help-333 or go to FastFreds.com.

Not only is this ad short and sweet, which allows us to run more ads for the same cost, but we have also increased the likelihood that our family man arriving home will scorn the Yellow Pages and simply dial HELP-333 or go to Fast Fred's web site.

As the detective you must now determine the POE for your own business. Here lies the real focus of an ad campaign.

I credit my discovery of this rule to a pet store owner in Jackson, Mississippi. His specialty was birds, especially parrots. His magic wand wish was to sell more parrots. There was a lot of profit in parrots. As a young-arrogant-know it all guru- I wasted no time in the detective process and just blurted out my brilliant solution. "We shall put together an ad to promote and sell parrots."

He was an older man, not in the best of health, and feeling rather poorly that day. But he patiently explained the concept of the point of entry.

"Don, you need to understand the point of entry. The parrot buyer is a middle aged man who has always wanted a parrot, but is afraid of the cost. He is also afraid of his wife who doesn't want the mess, or a bird that lives forever, or a bird that never gets past kindergarten language, or never gets a decent job, or never has grandchildren. So instead of advertising expensive parrots I advertise cheap little parakeets as the point of entry."

He gestured to a cage full of cute pink and blue parakeets for just five bucks each. Nearby was a foot-tall bright blue feathered, black beaked, yellow eyed parrot giving me a contemptuous look. His head rocked back and forth sideways as if to mock my ignorance. I could hear it thinking, "Tsssk, tsssk another cliché ridden stupid human…next thing he'll be asking me if I want a cracker."

I wagged my index finger at the bird and hissed at it to stop mocking me. I thought about offering it a cracker. The store owner intervened.

"Don you might be interested to know this is a rare and very old Hyacinth Macaw. He is worth about $10,000, as importing these guys has been illegal for some time. He can use that beak to crack open a coconut or bite off a cage bar, and if he gets a hold of your finger he'll snap it in two like a Popsicle stick."

As I dropped my wagging finger and as I backed slowly ever so slowly away from the parrot, the store owner made his desires clear...crystal clear.

"So Don, if you would, put together a commercial for me advertising five dollar parakeets as perfect pets for little kids. Aim it at middle aged man who has little kids. He will come in with the wife's blessing to get the kids a parakeet. Just get that guy in my store and I'll make sure he goes home with a parrot instead of a parakeet."

The point of entry rule was born on the spot.

The same point of entry issue applies to a lot of businesses. I sure hope you know what it is for your business.

Remember! It is the thing or the question or the reason people voice aloud the first time they enter your business.

If you do not know what it is, find out what it is by asking the person who takes incoming calls or greets new customers at the door. The receptionist or the person who answers the phone always knows.

If you can identify and focus on point of entry, a critical component of an ad campaign, your chances of achieving those illusive measurable results are certainly enhanced. Think about it!

Here's another example. I once counseled a brilliant tax attorney in San Francisco who worked with rich people who were being nailed by the IRS for things like blatant cheating on their taxes. To him, it seemed as if no amount of education or warnings about the consequences of cheating would do any good. And nobody called him until they were busted. Thus, he usually received calls on the day his potential clients were arrested or audited. They always asked the same question, "Can you keep me out of jail?"

His POE is obvious: Caught cheating on your taxes? Call me, Phil Finch, 678-3491 and save yourself some jail time.

RULE EIGHT:

SELLING OBVIOUS STUFF SINKS SALES

Dit Dit Dit, Dah Dah Dah, Dit Dit Dit, Dit Dit Dit, Dah Dah Dah, Dit Dit Dit. That's S.O.S. in Morse code.

For those lovers of disaster stories, you know that Morse code sequence was used on the night of April 14, 1912. It was transmitted soon after Captain E.J. Smith ordered, "Full ahead" in a crisp British accent and drove the *Titanic* into an iceberg just off the southeastern coast of Newfoundland.

The original meaning of the sequence three dots, three dashes and three dots meant Save Our Ship. However, as this book is about advertising, I'd like to assign a new meaning to S.O.S. That is Selling Obvious Stuff.

Selling Obvious Stuff in advertising can easily sink your business or at the very least, cause your advertising to fail, thus dooming you to the same fate as Captain Smith.

Since you're the captain of your ship, how can you avoid the perils of Selling Obvious Stuff, which all too often dooms advertising campaigns?

First, you need to know what the phrase means. Here's a real-life example to illustrate exactly what it is.

Consider a 30-second TV commercial run by Tommy's Travel Pros, a travel agency in Los Angeles, running a mid-summer campaign. The targeted audience is the stereotypical, office-worker drone whose hectic workday is compounded by traffic, a boorish boss, stress, kids at home and the like, all of which combine to allow barely enough time to shop for food, let alone to approach the significant other after the lights go off.

Tommy is trying to sell vacations.

On the TV, we see a sequence of standard vacation scenes:
- The deserted island beach in Fiji
- The family on a cruise ship
- Watching a bullfight in Spain
- Touring London in a double-decker bus

As we watch, the announcer is extolling the usual virtues of a vacation:
- Get away from the hassles of commuting
- Spend time with your family
- Relax with no office pressures
- Eat drink and be merry, for tomorrow you may be dead

Then at the end of the spot we are encouraged to call the travel experts at Tommy's Travel Pros for more information about that dream vacation.

Now ask yourself, what is the commercial selling? In other words, what is its main theme? From my perspective, I'd say it was attempting to sell the concept that taking a vacation is a good idea.

But stop right there. Isn't it inherently obvious that the office-worker drones already want a vacation? They're dreaming of a vacation. They're desperate for a vacation. They would kill for a vacation. So is there really a need to sell that concept?

No!! It's an obvious waste of time to sell something that needs no selling--a classic definition of Selling Obvious Stuff.

Even worse, assuming the ad does motivate someone to call and book a vacation, there is no guarantee Tommy's Travel Pros will get the business. There are, after all, gobs of agents in Los Angeles. What about the Internet? All those office drones have computers and they love to spend time in the middle of the day doing personal surfing. In fact, research tells us that the middle of the workday is the peak time for web shopping and planning things like vacations!

Fortunately, the solution is simple. Don't sell obvious stuff! The focus of the ad should instead be on getting people to call Tommy's or to visit Tommy's web site—and to never consider anyone else.

Here are some alternatives:

- Tommy's Travel Pros have the lowest rates on more tours to more cities in China.
- Tommy's Travel Pros specialize in luxury cruises to all four of the Hawaiian islands.
- When you book with Tommy's Travel Pros you get a free $10,000 travel insurance policy.
- At Tommy's Travel Pros we have agents who speak 35 different languages. Call us in any language.

Note that the previous examples focus on why viewers should call Tommy's, not on why they should take a vacation.

If that makes sense, let's take a look at how the Selling Obvious Stuff mistake can be made in other types of advertising and let's see how it can be corrected.

Obvious - The cosmetic dentist tells us we can have a nice healthy smile.

Corrected - The cosmetic dentist emphasizes his sedation technique which allows for a pain-free experience.

Obvious   - The hair-replacement clinic sells men on the concept of reversing their baldness.
Corrected - The hair-replacement clinic offers a private entrance and waiting rooms for those embarrassed by the whole process. It also has a web site you can visit in total privacy!

Obvious - The Indian casino selling the joy of winning.
Corrected - The Indian casino claiming a higher pay off rate on their slot machines than the competition.

Obvious - The hair-styling school sells the benefits of a career in hairdressing.
Corrected - The hair-styling school sells the 99.1% employment rate of its graduates.

Obvious - The Ford dealer sells the joy of a new mini-van for the family.
Corrected - The Ford dealer claims to be the mini-van king with more choices and more discounts on mini-vans.

One of the reasons the SOS rule has become even more critical in advertising is the Internet. A growing number of people search for goods and services on the Internet, making it the number one source of information for people shopping for obvious things like vacations, real estate, homes, cars, etc.

People are becoming more educated through the web, particularly when it comes to details about products and services. If the goal of your advertising is to drive traffic to your web site the SOS rule still applies. You must sell the specific reasons someone should visit your site beyond the obvious stuff. Let us revisit Tommy's Travel Pros for one more illustration of this rule as applied to driving web traffic.

Pushing the web site using obvious stuff – Visit Tommys.com for more information on vacations.

Pushing the web site by selling specifics – Look for the $1,000 coupon available this week at Tommys.com.

RULE NINE:

FOLLOW THE FOUR
FIDDLERS OF RETAIL

If the following statements apply, take note, because this chapter is written especially for you.

1. You have a lot of competitors.
2. Your competitors advertise heavily via electronic media, i.e. TV, radio, cable or the Internet.

As an example, take personal injury lawyers. Years ago there were no personal injury lawyers advertised on TV. Now it's the reverse. There are hundreds using TV, and many of them don't use printed ads. They spend their entire advertising budget on television. The first injury lawyers to shift to TV gained the most. It is worthwhile to note that for some reason lawyers do best with TV as opposed to radio. And conversely, there are businesses where radio seems to work better, such as concert ticket sales.

As technology has revolutionized the world of communications, so too has it revolutionized advertising. It is happening fast!

Let's just look at a few changes in what works and what fails. Prior to 2000 and particularly before 1990, advertising was a simpler concept to grasp. The rules, established back when Howdy Doody dominated Saturday TV and when everyone watched the network evening news, were different. To make my point, let's compare past advertising strategies to the present.

Then: Use a mix of good media, newspaper, solid radio stations and network TV.

Now: Unless you have the budget to utterly dominate all outlets, media mix is a death trap for local advertisers

Then: The message was not as important as the fact that you were visible. Most ads worked. If you were on radio in the 50s or TV in the 70s, you had to be the real deal. In those days, as Marshall McLuhan so eloquently pointed out, "The medium is the message."

Now: Marshall McLuhan is dead and so is his quote. Today the better quote is mine: "The message is the message."

Then: Bland generic ads that simply touted your name and your reputation worked.

Now: To break through the clutter, ads need to be unique and specific with a call to action.

Then: Far fewer satellite networks, fewer cable channels. Fewer radio stations. No Internet. Newspaper alive and well. Choosing a good media partner was certainly much easier

Now: Choosing the right place to advertise is now much harder

Enter the new world order, a world where new is old in shorter and shorter periods of time. It is a world in which the advertising process is dynamic, changing and ever more challenging, if you want measurable results from your advertising.

In this new world, measurable results, for those of you who have many competitors using the electronic media to advertise, have an especially difficult challenge. We have all seen nine billion car dealer, furniture store and retail ads in every niche from fast food to local lawyers. For those of you who face this kind of challenge, I have invented the next rule.

The rule of the four fiddlers of retail:

Each hypothetical fiddler has his own sweet song (lesson) to play. We will examine them individually. However, it is the incorporation of all four lessons together that works best in a crowded and highly competitive advertising environment. So in your ads, include the lessons from each of them.

The first fiddler is consistent. He plays the same song over and over, but he breaks out of the pack with a twist of some kind.

Let's look at a car dealer who does his own ads all the time. He becomes the consistent identity. But if he just does the standard walk up and down the rows of cars or blabs on the radio about his great deals, there is no twist. There is nothing to make his ads look or sound different.

Add in shots or sounds of him riding a bull, playing drums, singing his commercial or reporting from a helicopter above the dealership and now we have a twist to make him stand out from dozens of other dealers.

The use of animals illustrates the same concept of consistency with a twist. The Aflac duck and the GEICO gecko are national examples, but the concept can easily be copied locally. One of my local favorites is a southern car dealer who claims to be "the Big Dog for Trucks." His consistent spokes-animal is a Great Dane who speaks perfect English.

In the broader category of consistency the point remains the same. Pick something with a twist and stay with it.

Animation also works well. Locally, I have seen hand-held puppets, a talking house, tires that bounce and sing and even cute, little, talking, four-month-old babies with Italian accents.

The second fiddler is a musician who stakes out a niche in one specialty, rather than playing country music, opera and the blues all in one gig.

In the old days you could cover a laundry list of products and services as discussed in previous chapters. Today, you would look at what you have to offer and stake a claim to some unique position or niche for that product or service.

For some, staking out a niche is easy. If you're a swimming pool dealer, the product niche is swimming pools. But if you're located in Las Vegas and competing with 50 other pool people you need something really unique. For example:

"The fastest swimming pool installer in Las Vegas"
"The lowest priced pools"
"Specialists in luxury pools"
"The only dealer in San Juan fiberglass pools"
"Home of the $99-a-month swimming pool"

"We offer more choices in design and size than anyone else"

Keep the second fiddler in mind as you settle on your unique claim. Remember, your claim has to be specific and easily understood as to why it sets you apart from your competitors. Claiming to be all things to all people rarely works in advertising today.

The third fiddler is the one who can take requests and play a thousand different songs.

In the retail world, you must demonstrate in your ads that you have a large selection and lots of choices. Keep in mind that shoppers visit fewer stores than they did years ago. For example, in the highly competitive category of furniture, just a decade ago the typical shopper would visit maybe five stores. Today, consumers visit fewer than two. It's the same with car dealers, jewelry stores and swimming pool dealers. Visiting fewer stores is due to a combination of no time to shop in stores and lots of time to shop on the Internet.

Here is a story I hear over and over all across America. Most shopping decisions and most purchase decisions in

America today are made by women. The number reported to me by most retailers is 70 percent. The fate of most car dealers, schools, hospitals, funeral homes, drug stores, vacation destinations, home builders, dentists and just about every category known to man is now controlled by women.

Women love to shop and increasingly they do it on the Internet. Let's toss out another number. It's 70 percent again. This time it reflects the percentage of women who have educated themselves and shopped for what they want on the Internet, before they set one pointy-toed shoe in any store. Then when they do visit your store they already know what they want. They know what color. What style. What price. And if your store does not carry enough selection to have what they want, they will go elsewhere.

Consider a Volkswagen dealer who has a customer walk in, refuse a test drive and state the facts: "I want a new VW Jetta with a five speed and the turbo, in white with a sunroof. I'll pay you exactly $22,348 financed over 48 months with no money down and a payment of $431 a month and that must include taxes and title and all delivery charges. Deal or no deal?"

Can you guess when and where most of this Internet shopping and education is occurring? By web click statistics, most action occurs (choose one):

a) At home during major TV sporting events
b) At work during lunch hours and coffee breaks
c) At home prior to the holiday season
d) In the office during prime workday hours

Yep! The answer is the last one.

The web era has created a new nightmare for stores that are number three or four in a category where selection is key. As shoppers now do their initial homework online, they visit fewer stores to make the purchase. They usually go to the one or two stores with greater selection. If you are number three or four on the list you never get visited.

The fourth fiddler plays in the band but sells the tickets at the door.

The fourth fiddler gets people in front of the stage. To sell tickets, a call to action or some incentive to use a service, buy an item or use a business is a must for any competitive ad. But before you go off the deep end and think that only price-cuts work, take heart that there are many variations of the call to action. Take a look at some examples below and pick the one that's right for you.

- Come in this weekend and sample some authentic East Indian tea along with fresh baked crumpets as you consider your purchase at Rolls Royce of Miami.

- Once a year, our diamond buyers return from Amsterdam with some really special one karat sizes, but it's first-come, first-served at Import Jewelers.

- The new Harold Hammer book is on sale for just $14.95 this Friday afternoon for three hours with a live book signing by Hammer himself.

- It's a factory authorized sale on Merilat Kitchen Cabinets, which could save you as much as $5,000 on your kitchen remodeling. Miss this and you miss the bargain of the year at King Kitchens.

- It's an emergency liquidation sale (add in some sirens) at Billy Bob's Sports. Billy is in trouble with the bank and needs an emergency infusion of cash. Prices slashed up to 60 percent now!

A real-life example of the four fiddlers in action:

Allow me to relate a real-life story to illustrate how important it is to include all the four fiddlers in order to make an ad that produces measurable results. In this case, I wrote an ad for a big car dealer in a large Florida market. Naturally I wrote what I thought was a great ad.

The first fiddler: For a consistent spokesperson with a twist, I went for a lady helicopter pilot, complete with leather jacket and scarf, who broadcasts from a helicopter hovering above the dealership. Not your standard stand-up guy in a sport jacket blabbing in front of a row of cars.

The second fiddler: The unique position or niche was made abundantly clear. The claim we staked out was that of used car superstore.

The third fiddler: Then we really hit on the huge selection of used cars the dealership offered by making it clear that there were 450 used cars on the lot.

The fourth fiddler: To get them in the door, I suggested a weekend sale on all the used trucks in stock.

The result? It failed miserably. The dealer cancelled in exactly six weeks. What happened? Was I no longer a Guru? Had my powers been robbed by some strange Floridian force?

Why did it fail? Was it me? Let's see.

No, it was not me. It was the dealer who decided to leave out one of the fiddlers. He cut out the call to action and decided to go without the weekend sale I had suggested. The gnarly finger of blame thus points directly at his head, not mine.

RULE TEN:

TAGS ARE FOR DOGS

Cool title for a chapter. Don't you agree? But what does it
mean?

We are talking about the wretched practice of running
factory ads with a tag allowed for the local retailer. It's
called co-op advertising. It is a commercial paid for in part
by the factory and in part by you. It allows you to promote
both the big national name and your local store in one spot
with the cost shared equally between you and the factory.

But all you get is a tag … and I believe tags are for dogs. Let's look at a specific real-life example to discuss the point.

Here is an actual 30-second co-op commercial. The names have been changed to protect the proverbial innocent, namely myself, from litigators who would crush me like a peanut shell on a bar floor if I used real product or business identities.

Visualize:

A beautiful king-sized bed lit by the soft light of dawn filtering through a picture window. Butterflies flutter around a vase of morning lilies on a nearby dresser.

In the background, you hear the Mormon Tabernacle Choir singing a blissful, comforting lullaby.

Comfortably arrayed, surrounded by warm quilts and fluffy pillows, a perfect couple lays asleep, blissfully smiling, arms around each other.

A giant woolly sheep with the number 26 spray painted on its side and brandishing really big horns stands at the foot of their bed.

The sheep softly bleats a staccato Se-r-r-r-r-r-r-pa, as an announcer extols the virtues of the Serpa Bedding System, upon which the couple sleeps luxuriously.

For the final five seconds, the following tag appears on a white screen:

Ralph's Mattress Outlet
657 Fourth Street
567-5646
www.ralphforless.com

The ad is filmed to perfection and looks fabulous on the screen. Although only 30 seconds long, it must have cost thousands to produce. Now here is the big question. If Ralph's paid 50 percent of costs for the ad and Serpa Bedding paid the other half, did Ralph get a good deal?

Let's do the math.

The 25-second sequence with the couple in bed was all about the Serpa Bedding System, which means Serpa got 83 percent of the air time versus Ralph's 17 percent for his 5 seconds. So, if they split the cost, then something is dramatically wrong with this deal!

But wait, it gets worse--for Ralph that is. You see, he happens to be in a large competitive market where not one, not two, not three, but four other stores sell the exact same Serpa Bedding System.

That wretched five-second tag at the end of the ad could just as easily send a viewer to one of his competitor's stores as to Ralph's. In fact, tragically Ralph is actually advertising for his competitors as well.

Of course there may be exceptions. For example, let's assume that Ralph's is the only store in town, or within 100 miles, that sells the Serpa Bedding System. Under those circumstances, Ralph is obviously not advertising for his competitors.

But he is still paying 50 percent of the cost for a mere 17 percent of air time.

Hence my title: Tags (i.e. co-op) Are For Dogs.

If you find yourself in a similar inequitable circumstance like Ralph, justice may be served by taking some easy, common sense steps.

Call the factory rep and find out what you can do to produce your own ad. With few exceptions, most factory reps will allow you to produce your own ad with some basic requirements and you will get the 50 percent co-op. You may have to mention the factory's name four times, show their logo or make some branding statement, but then you are free to promote yourself. We want to flip the costs so you pay 50 percent of the cost and get 83 percent of the ad content.

There's one drawback. Over the years co-op has become harder to get and there are some manufacturers who are draconian in their demands. That is, they require that you use their production. Fortunately, they are in the minority and most of the others will work with you. Just make sure you are aware of their guidelines.

Let's take a look at what happens when we get permission to produce an ad locally. First, we rewrite the ad for Ralph and show how easy it is to not only get the co-op but to also get a lot more airtime for his business.

Second, we produce the ad locally. The quality is good for local production, but lacks that polished nationally made quality. "Hey," you say, "isn't that a bad thing?"

NO! I stand up and say, "Hallelujah! Fabulous! Fantastic!" I want Ralph's production to look like a local ad. Why? Because locally produced ads for local businesses work better!

This is worth repeating. I often hear people expressing the desire to develop ads that are up to national production standards. Yet the most successful ads are often ones that are locally made. Modern television and sound systems, prevalent in almost all TV and radio stations, virtually ensures high-quality picture and sound.

So, given that you are assured of a well-produced ad, technologically speaking, you know that it's the message that will dictate its success or failure. Of course, there are exceptions. Particular attention to production techniques is needed for the local, high-end jewelers, funeral homes and hospitals. But the everyday flower shops, convenience stores, electricians, furniture stores, car dealers and mom-and-pop stores seem to get better results from normal self-production methods.

Keeping that in mind, with permission from the Serpa factory, let's now rewrite the ad for Ralph's.

Now visualize:

The scene opens in Ralph's showroom, his logo plainly visible on the wall, along with that of the Serpa Bedding Systems.

The camera narrows to a shot of a couple asleep on one of the beds.

As the narrator details Ralph's showroom, it becomes apparent that one of the heads on the pillow belongs to Ralph and the other is that of a large stuffed Tibetan sheep. Ralph awakens and sleepily tells us that he loves selling the Serpa Bedding System because nothing delivers a better night's rest. In fact, right now he's offering a clearance special on all queen-sized Serpa beds.

The narrator repeats the queen-sized Serpa bed clearance specials and then asks Ralph to explain the presence of the goat in the bed.

Ralph pulls out the stuffed sheep and tells us that he's giving away a free stuffed Serpa sheep with each queen-sized Serpa bed sold this weekend.

Then, to make damn sure Ralph's competitors don't benefit from his advertising dollar, the ad ends again with five seconds on Ralph's name, location and now, slogan, "Ralph's is THE best place in the state to buy a Serpa Bedding System."

The changes above are obvious. There's a lot more about Ralph's in the rewritten version.

So before we conclude, let's take a closer look at a technique that many producers use when ending an ad; a technique, which more often than not, causes "Advert Mortus" (advertising death).

Have you ever taken an existing ad and "tagged" it with additional information, such as:

"Don't forget our holiday hours are now 8am to 8pm except Sunday, noon to 6."

"Be sure to visit our new location at the Greendale Mall right next to Spencer's Furniture"

"Visit us on the web at www.wilsonsports.com."

"For directions, hours of operation, call us during business hours at 788-9900."

Ah my children, I hear your confessions and I admire your ability to recognize the sins of the past. But don't ever do it again. Here's why. That pathetic little five-second tag is going to be missed by your customers anyway. It's invisible. It's a tiny voice from the upper level of Yankee Stadium that nobody hears.

If the content of the tag is really important to you, make it the focus of the entire commercial and don't mess around thinking you have covered all your bases with the tag.

For example, right now the web site is a critical issue for many of us. If you want people on your web site, either devote the entire ad to promoting it (this works very well for used car dealers, realtors, retailers, etc. who have lots of details, education and explanations to get across) or put the web site address at the bottom of the screen of your ad for the entire 30 seconds. If it's a radio ad, hammer it home at least six times in a 60-second ad.

Let's finish our time in the confessional with two other pet topics of mine. This may induce further pain for you, but remember, it's a healing process.

First, crawls. Think CNN, FOX and just about every other national news site that uses crawls. Ever read them? Better yet, have you ever put a crawl at the bottom of your ad? Sob. I confess I have. More sobs. It was years ago and I was young and stupid. When I stuck that crawl on the bottom of the ad I immediately took the viewer's eye to the crawl and of course off of the main body of the ad. If tags are for dogs, crawls are for rattle snakes. They may get your attention but everything else disappears from view.

Last is national footage. Have you ever used it in your advertising?

You know, those beautiful polished production clips you get from the national marketing department. The Ford F-

150, for example, charges around the curves of Mount Everest as it climbs to the peak in a blizzard. Or the beautiful diamond sparkles as it rotates on a green velvet pedestal in some exotic museum.

Here's the problem with using national footage. The producers of these ads are selling their product, not you or your business. Insert that clip of the F-150 in your ad and you are promoting Ford F-150s for every Ford dealer in your market. Show the gorgeous diamonds on the pedestal and you are promoting the concept of diamonds and the dozens of stores in your market that carry diamonds.

If you have done it in the past your penance is simple: don't do it again. We want to always promote you, your business and the reasons why anyone should buy from you. Period! As opposed to the thieving scurrilous inferior lackeys with whom you compete for survival.

RULE ELEVEN:

TEST DRIVE THE AD

For sale: Used elephant. One owner since birth. 1964 model. Perfect health. De-tusked. Certified rage-free. Great for logging, short trips to the market and stomping out anthills or annoying neighbors. Obeys commands in three languages including English.

Assuming you wanted this elephant would you buy it without taking a test drive? Doubtful. Yet we constantly air new ads without testing their ability to deliver results.

One of the huge advantages national ad agencies have over local advertisers is their ability to test drive their commercials before they hit the air. They call it a focus group.

Simply put, they have test individuals view and give their reaction to a commercial before it is publicly aired. Naturally, these advertising agencies know knowledge is power and in this instance it also saves a load of money. The concept seems fairly simple and effective and, amazingly so, it is.

An ad is previewed by a demographically appropriate focus group, i.e. individuals consisting of the target customer age, sex, social status, income, education, etc. Reactions are noted, changes are made if necessary, and the ad is tuned to become as effective as possible.

Conceivably, the creators of the Aflac duck commercial were quite hesitant when that ad was first previewed. But when a focus group revealed an immediate attachment to the duck, even old-school conservatives of the American Family Life Assurance Company were ready to run that ultimately hugely successful ad campaign.

Let's look at the Aflac campaign a little more. Prior to the duck the company was spending $60 million a year advertising in sundry media outlets, which resulted in public name recognition of approximately 12 percent. The Aflac duck campaign concentrated that entire amount in electronic media, specifically television, and within one year the company had close to 90 percent name recognition. Note, it wasn't just the duck that led to the phenomenal success of this ad but also the fact that the entire ad budget was concentrated into one outlet.

Sound familiar? You heard me preach about media concentration back in chapter 6. Give credit to the marketing genius of the ad agency, The Kaplan Thaler Group and they didn't even use my book.

Dominating in radio The Richards Advertising Group conducted an equally successful campaign for Motel 6 with Tom Boudett's, "We'll leave the light on for you," which I guarantee was also tested.

Now let's go back to the local market, where financial realities usually preclude the use of full-blown focus groups. What to do?

Fortunately, there's an easy, no-cost solution requiring very little time or energy. It's called a field test. You simply take an ad and show it to someone within your target demographic. You don't give a rat's whisker if they like your ad or not. Remember chapter one: Liking or disliking an ad has nothing to do with its success. You are simply testing to see what message they get from the ad. (Of course, you pray that that message matches your Magic Wand wish.)

I learned to field test in Portland, Maine in 1982. I was working on a billboard campaign and had just completed a two-by-three-foot mock-up of an ad for my radio station. Naturally, I was delighted with my creation and was sure that it would be a great success. However, the artist I hired to finish the final version was a lot older and wiser than me. He sagely suggested I take the mock-up, walk out onto Congress Street and ask passersby what the billboard meant to them.

So I confidently approached the middle-class, middle-aged-looking women walking by; as this was the targeted new audience I was trying to attract for my radio station, KISS 100 FM. I skipped on the homeless lady going through the nearby dumpster. Back then, Portland was far from a tourist Mecca.

That was my first experience with field-testing. I'll get back to the results shortly.

First it's important to note that anyone can field test almost any type of commercial. You don't even need to leave the building. Just grab someone who is unfamiliar with what you are advertising and ask them: What message do you get from this commercial?

Hopefully, they will repeat back the Magic Wand wish.

Pretend for a moment you are putting together a campaign for a divorce attorney. You know the Magic Wand wish is that anyone involved in a custody battle should call your firm.

The television ad you create is powerful. It shows a man and woman pulling on the arms of a child as the narrator confidently assures the viewer that the custody battle can be won. The radio version is similar except we hear the poor kid's crying in the background.

Field-testing the ad is simple. Find someone in the middle of a divorce. Let them watch or listen to your proposed ad and determine what message they get.

Ideally the test subject says that they believe your firm is the place to go for a divorcing parent caught in a custody battle. If so, you can air the ad with the additional assurance that it should generate results, an assurance provided by an easy, inexpensive field test.

So how about my billboard field test for that radio station? My design consisted of a red lipstick mark next to the words KISS 100 FM, a picture of a radio dial set at 100, the actual call letters WKYS and finally the large words "Relaxing Music."

As I made my way up and down the street, I was stunned to get these interpretations:

"It's an ad for those cute little Hershey Kisses."
(*What?*)

"A new lipstick."

(*What? What?*)

"A Valentine's Day promotion."

(*It was April at the time.*)

"Isn't FM a new type of music?"

(*Remember, this was 1982.*)

"Ecch! I hate that lipstick."

(*So did I, but the boss chose it.*)

I dejectedly returned to the artist and started over. It was clear my billboard had failed the field test. The artist, without much gloating, informed me of the famous billboard rule: "Anything over seven words will fail, especially when seen from a moving car." The resulting remake? No graphics, just these words in huge type:

NEW RADIO STATION
100.1 ON FM DIAL

Armed with a whole new attitude about my potential listeners, the next field test attracted comments like:

"A new station? Should I try it?"

(*That's why we're advertising!*)

"It's a new FM station?

(Well Duhhhhh!)

"I wonder what kind of music they play."

(I used up my 7 words already)

"Is it new?"

(No, we put the word "new" there just for fun)

"A new FM station? I'll give it a try. We need more choices."

(I love you!)

That copy made the actual billboard.

As a side note, in the web era, billboards have enjoyed a surge of new business from those who want to promote their web sites. The same rules of simplicity apply. Those who just put up their web site will win. *WeGrowHair.Com* is plastered all over billboards in Nashville, Tennessee right now and I bet it works because those words occupy the entire board. Those who must add in more copy points will fail.

In ending, let me add three final warnings about field-testing.

First: If the ad is not crystal clear you will get all kinds of weird interpretations. If the copy can't be understood by a seven-year-old it probably won't work.

Second: Be especially careful when choosing co-workers to screen ads for sensitive topics, such as alcohol rehab programs, obesity clinics or cosmetic dental surgeons. They may take offense.

Third, if your ad is written with the express purpose of driving traffic to your web site make sure to apply the same field-testing strategies on a computer. Ask your guinea pig to find the web site, open it up and click around. The point is exactly the same. You want to see if they understand how to find your site and what they do when they get there. If they go to a search engine like Google or Yahoo and can't find you quickly, it is doom. If they have to click a lot of buttons or get lost navigating your site, it's double doom.

RULE TWELVE:

THE NEED FOR SPEED

Most people today are aware that there just isn't enough time to do everything. Perhaps an old episode from the great series <u>The Twilight Zone</u> had the best solution to this dilemma. In the episode the main character discovers a stopwatch with supernatural power. All he has to do is hit the stop button and the entire world freezes in time, except of course him. Then he just punches the button to start it again. Who wouldn't want that kind of time control?

Unfortunately our main character misuses the watch, stops the world while he robs a bank and ironically breaks the watch making his escape. He still roams alone in a world frozen in time forever, an excessive solution to be sure.

You and I wouldn't rob banks, would we? But we surely would stop time to extend the vacation, get more done, avoid red lights, etc. We're all busy. So let's examine the effect this has on the advertising strategies we use in our businesses.

The most obvious effect is the required inclusion of the word "fast" or the implication of some time savings for the customer, in most advertising. Fast food, fast delivery, fast service, fast whatever has been with us forever and has spawned the requisite changes in the way we do business. The drive-up window is one obvious example.

In my countrywide visits I see an expansion of businesses that have played the "fast" card with great success, especially in the service industries. GEICO says, "Give us 15 minutes, and we will save you 15 percent." Enterprise says, "Call us and we'll pick you up right away."

And locally there's the plumber who claims same-day service, the air-conditioning repairman who claims the one-hour response, the 10-minute oil change and the car dealer promising instant delivery of your new car.

I have often suggested integrating the "fast" philosophy into advertising whenever possible, particularly because it is a brilliant counter to serious competition.

One of my favorite ads was for an MRI imaging center in Lawton, Oklahoma. Their competition was a highly regarded hospital equipped with the latest technology. But that hospital was also big, replete with the massive parking lot, mazes of white-walled corridors and the Gestapo like nurses hidden behind frosted glass windows which were always in the shut position. There were at least two or three of those checkpoints to clear before you even sat down in the waiting room to read old issues of large print *Reader's Digest.*

The campaign we ran for our imaging center was "Home of the No Waiting Room!" The ad showed patients parking at the door, walking straight to their guaranteed, on-time appointments while being told, "We don't have waiting rooms here because we see you on time every time." It was a resounding success.

Often overlooked by those of us who write ads is the need for speed in delivering the actual message. Time-starved customers are also becoming less and less tolerant of long messages that don't deliver information fast. Let me clarify the mental state of the typical audience today as regards to the length of commercials.

I'll make this sweet, short and fast because you want sweet, short and fast. You neeeeeed sweet, short and fast. You demand sweet, short and fast, and if you don't get sweet, short and fast, you are going to get angry. You're getting annoyed at this repetitive use of short, sweet and fast, aren't you? I'm wasting your time, aren't I? You're getting mad as hell and you are not going to take it much longer, are you? Now imagine the response of viewers and listeners to the typical ads they are constantly subjected to. For example:

1. The 60-second blah blah blah radio commercials. Today, 60 seconds is like a day in line at the bank, if the ad doesn't hold your listener's interest. For radio, I am totally in favor of a 30-second ad, and if we can get the Magic

Wand wish accomplished in 20, 15 or even 5 seconds, all the better. In that case, your budget also benefits--more spots, more frequency and correspondingly, more results.

2. The 30-second blah blah blah TV spot is equally intolerable. If we can get the Magic Wand wish accomplished in 20, 15 or even 5 seconds, go for it. Use the money saved to buy more spots.

3. Anything that doesn't get straight to the point. Today, you simply can't afford to slowly get to the point of "What's in it for the customer?" You'd best tell them your point right out of the gate. At the very least, use something short that demands their undivided attention and then move to "What's in it for the customer."

Here's proof of my claim about the 60 second radio commercial. (I bet you won't take the time to read it all.)

Announcer: When Dr. Bob Billmont founded St. Sebastian's Hospital for Women back in 1896, he was a pioneer in the field of care for women, and especially for those having babies. Today, St. Sebastian's has grown to a staff of 170 dedicated staff members. For doctors, nurses, medical assistants, technicians, and all of St. Sebastian's health care providers, the mission is one and the same: "Serving the health care needs of our community, one family at a time." If you or someone you know is preparing to start a family of her own or increase the family size with another addition, we invite you to consider St. Sebastian's and their state-of-the-art birthing center. You can schedule a tour anytime by calling the birthing center at 667-7777, extension 1045. Tours are given on Sundays and Mondays. When you are expecting a baby you have a lot of decisions to make and we hope that one of them will be to choose St. Sebastian's. By the way, if you don't have good insurance or a lot of cash, call the public hospital across town instead. They still take charity cases and cheapskate chiselers. (Ok, that's there to see who really read the whole ad.) Once again, remember you can schedule a tour anytime by calling the birthing center at 667-7777, extension 1045. That's 667-7777, extension 1045.

Here is how you might reduce this to a 30-second radio ad and get more calls.

Woman: Oh my ...I'm pregnannnnnnt!
Doctor: I'm Dr. Mary Murphy at St. Sebastian's. After you find out the wonderful news, please call, ask for me

and let us give you a personal guided tour of St. Sebastian's birthing center. Or visit our web site for a virtual tour. Not only will you find out why St. Sebastian's, located right here in Missoula, is the best facility in the state to have your baby, we can explain our special cooperative program with State University, which provides tuition assistance for college if you have your baby with St. Sebastian's.
Woman: The best birthing center in the state and tuition assistance for college--what a great way to bring your baby into the world!

In this case, phone numbers and web site addresses are not needed in the radio ad because St. Sebastian's is a name everyone knows in a small town like Missoula, Montana.

I could write forever on time and its huge impact on advertising. People shop fewer stores than ever. People punch out of commercials faster than ever. People who work have no time to read the daily paper (if they even subscribe to one).

When it comes to the time trap, the web gets an exception with some hooks. People will indeed spend more time on individual web pages but here is the big hook. They will not tolerate complicated sites. Right now, the web people say anything that takes more than three clicks to get to the desired page is too much. An opening page loaded with text of the blah blah blah nature is just as bad on the home page as blah blah blah in TV or radio. Give them a nice menu to choose from and save the text and explanations for the specific pages in which they have serious interest.

And yes even you reading this book, you want to move on as fast as possible. I understand grasshopper. Let us jump to the next chapter.

RULE THIRTEEN:

CHEESE TO CHEESE
STEAK TO STEAK

Let's begin with a reading assignment. Take a look at the following excerpt from a daily newspaper and see if you understand it:

Τρομοκράτες τρίτης γενιάς
Αλλες επτά ρουκέτες αχρησιμοποίητες στα χέρια τους

Δέκα εισαγγελείς σε επιφυλακή για τις έρευνες * Τι φοβάται η κυβέρνηση * Το «φάντασμα του Θαπατέρο» πάνω από το Μαξίμου * Ποιους υποψιάζεται η Αστυνομία Τρομοκράτες τρίτης γενιάς - μετά τον ΕΛΑ και τη 17Ν - βρίσκονται πίσω από το

I don't know about you, but it looks like Greek to me. Wait a minute, it is Greek! And obviously, if you don't understand the language, you can't understand the message! On the other hand, if you want to reach the Greeks, this is the language of choice, isn't it?

In advertising, we have to speak in the language or culturally accepted communication style of our intended customer.

In France nudity is socially accepted in TV commercials. A great billboard campaign some years back promoted a perfume by featuring a fully clothed woman, who then lost one item of clothing each week in a gradual striptease until she was naked.

In Saudi Arabia a sexual display of that kind could literally cause the advertiser to lose his or her head.

In Russia they'd say it's too cold to dress like that.

Okay, it's easy to make my point using foreign cultures, but let's make it a little more practical. Let's shift to America and ask if commercials written in English are easier to understand. After all, English is English isn't it?

I say no. Advertisements written in English do not and can not have the same meaning to everyone. I've seen and experienced it constantly in areas with high populations of first-and second-generation foreign immigrants who speak limited English. Sometimes this cultural filter can even complicate the Guru's rules. For example, some of the clichés that I have condemned as overused, such as "family owned" or "you can trust us," may actually work with a particular group of people, such as first- and second-generation Hispanic immigrants, because statistically they still have a high regard for media and its commercials.

Ultimately, word choice, usage, word order, grammar and the individuality of the audience determine whether or not your message is received, much less understood.

As a result, it's difficult to figure out how an ad will be interpreted even when it's written in English.

For example, take this simple 10-second ad:

Need a used car? You can trust Honest Joe to sell you a good, safe used car! Right now, Joe has 10 cars on the lot, priced to go at just $99 down and $99 a month. Come on in today. Visit Joe on Route 1 right next to the Westgate Mall.

Seems simple enough, but does it have the same meaning to all people? Here are some possible interpretations.

To one of Joe's loyal, old, happy customers, the ad seems to say, "Yeah, you gotta love Joe. He sells good stuff, cheap!"

To a middle-class, working woman from the suburbs, the ad may be viewed quite differently: "Are you kidding me? If I went down there, I'd be assaulted or robbed. That's the wretched side of town!"

To a counter-culture, 21-year-old college student, it prompts the feeling that "Joe is surely a thief and a liar. In fact, all ads today are a pack of lies."

Use the language your targeted audience uses. Cheese to cheese and steak to steak.

If you're writing an ad designed to attract hardworking, middle-aged, blue-collar workers, write in language they understand. They might like the cheese. If high-end, Wall Street lawyers are your target, you may need to use different language. They might like the steak.

Test your grasp of this rule.

Can you write a commercial for a party supply store that is trying to attract a 13-year-old girl and her mom planning a birthday party? I can't. I don't know that language. I'm past 60, my grandson Jack is only five months old, so teenage girls and their mothers are out of my realm.

Can you write an ad for a senior citizen like me, who has committed his life to shaving three strokes off his golf handicap and defeating his neighbor the doctor, who is also a natural athlete and an ex-division one basketball player? A man who I have never beat at anything! Maybe you can't write that ad, but you bet I can!! I already speak that language and I'll buy anything that promises a lower golf score or enhances my chances of defeating him. I'll even buy a book like "Anything to Win," and a subtitle of "Defeating your lifelong opponent with underhanded tricks and mind games!" Now that's written in a language I understand.

Cheese to cheese. Pretend you are a lawyer seeking inquiries for personal injury claims. Can you write a cheesy ad for a low life who loves Jerry Springer and is home at 3pm with a Bud Light in hand? That's a pure cheese sell. My personal favorite in that category has nothing to do with legal expertise or the law. No, it's as simple as "Had a wreck? Get a check!"

Steak to steak. But what about the other end of the spectrum? Let's look at the exclusive housing development on the good side of town. Our commercial here is more refined, subtle and presented in a different style: "A few select homes of distinction are now being offered for sale to those who appreciate a gated community." In the language of steak people the meaning is clear; we keep the riff-raff at a discreet distance.

And the appropriate language to reach the under 30 generation, especially the males, is really tough. This demographic scorns most standard ads. I do not know how to write for them.

I was in upstate New York making a presentation to a beer distributor who wanted some promotion ideas for Pabst Blue Ribbon beer.

The standard message used by the big ad agencies for beer products usually include words such as "light," "crisp" or "refreshing." Take a look at most beer bottle labels.

Pabst, however, is very popular with college kids. So I decided to ask my youngest son, Jamie, then in college at the University of Massachusetts, to tell me why. Just by asking him that one simple question, I learned one of the all-time greatest potential ad lines (never used) for selling beer to college kids.

Jamie answered, "TCBTGUD" with great enthusiasm and a fist pump.

"What?"

"It's pronounced, Ta CiB Ta GUD!" He replied.

"What?" I asked. Not knowing the language I was more confused than ever.

"TCBTGUD," he repeated, as if it would help.

"What?" I was getting frustrated at that point.

"The Cheap Beer That Gets U Drunk."

I would also suggest you apply this cheese-to-cheese, steak-to-steak concept when choosing a web name. In Las Vegas, I met with a fertility clinic that chose a web name that utilized the perfect language to speak to women trying to get pregnant: *iwantababy.com*. Even better, when you clicked on their site, they added in another powerful woman-to-woman message: "All of our staff and doctors are female."

There are a thousand different languages out there.

College kid to college kid.
Wanna-be mom to wanna-be mom.
Steak to steak.
Cheese to cheese.

Your homework assignment is to identify and study the one language which reaches your core customers.

RULE FOURTEEN:

HIRE LOCAL TALENT

Some of us have great television charisma and personality. Some of us have awesome radio voices. Some of us can sing and others can dance. But it's a cold fact that some of us have none of the above. This harsh fact of life hasn't stopped many business owners from doing his or her own advertisements.

Why do they do it? They do it for consistency, to save money, for pride or ego, or because it works even if they are horrid. Still others, for various reasons, refuse to do ads themselves.

This chapter is written for the others—those business owners who seek and use the talent of others for their advertising.

At first glance, employees seem to be a perfectly suited resource, but alas, they quit at times, get fired or may even be caught embezzling. It's happened to all of us!

My favorite employee story comes from a cable TV system in Louisiana that often used one particular sales lady in many of their ads. Years later, I heard she went to prison after being convicted for running an illegal "escort service for men." As the head madam she had been using the cable system as a front.

I have discovered a great alternative to appearing in your own ads, using employees or even family members. It's easy, surprisingly inexpensive and almost guaranteed to produce professional results.

Hire local talent.

There are talented actors right under your nose and they should be easy to find without engaging an expensive talent or booking agency. I'm talking about a previously untapped resource: the local artistic talent who frequent the community theatres and music stores all across the fruited plains of America.

Virtually every town, university and high school has a local theater group; individuals who get together to put on plays or performances for the local citizenry. Their talent is often amazing, and they're delighted for any opportunity to act, especially in advertisements.

Costs for a typical ad utilizing this resource vary and are negotiable, ranging from an average of $50 or $100 in small- to medium-sized markets, to $200 in bigger markets.

One auto dealer I visited recruited an entire high-school marching band for their commercial for no cost. The high school loved the publicity, as did the 75 happy parents who watched their kids on television, not to mention the 75 likely car buyers in the near future.

Looking for that fresh, perfect voice? Just search the web for "announcers" or "voices." You will find a variety of Internet-based talent houses charging small fees for the voice of your choice. You send them your copy, and it's returned within 24 hours, all via the Internet.

Another way to explain my prejudice toward local talent is to cite some real-life questions I fielded from a jewelry store owner in downtown Rochester, New York. Let us call him Ted!

Q. I want my ad to have a national look or sound. Can the local station really deliver highly polished production or talent? My jewelry store needs a very high-end image.

A. Ted, today the technology has advanced so far that almost all your local stations and cable systems have the digital cameras and editing equipment capable of a national look, if that is what you really want.

Q. What do you mean, if that is what I really want? Hey, I'm one of the last surviving local jewelers competing with all the national chains at the mall and strip-mall stores. My ads have to look as good as theirs.

My diamonds have to sparkle and shine as I show off their brilliancy, their cut, their color and their clarity. It's all about CCC!

A (My mental answer). No, actually, Ted, I think that CCC stuff is out-dated fodder from some gem institute and means nothing to anyone today. It's blah blah blah, when the real issue to most women is size and price. Save that boring lecture for your web site.

A (My actual answer). Most consumers think that the higher the production values, the more expensive the product or service. The jewelry store with the snottiest commercial, reeking of brilliant production, fantastic lighting and camera work, will send out a message of high price.

Q. What if I want to be the high-priced jeweler serving the wealthy and the elite with bigger profit margins to boot?

A. Then I'll agree with you. Is that what you want?

Q. Actually, no. I already have an image as very high priced. And my wealthy and elite old customers are

dying off. I need younger, but the younger women scorn downtown stores like mine. In truth, I have a downtown store with virtually no rent and I can beat all other jewelry stores on price and selection every day because I have the lowest overhead in the market, yet I'm losing business to them.

A. Hire local talent. Use local production. I suggest that we get a local woman who can act the role of a newly engaged 25-year-old, put her on camera in our well-lit studio with a nice, simple background. Let her tell the world that she discovered that your downtown store could sell a better diamond for less money than those big national chains at the malls. The cost for her will be about $50. The studio production, which will look totally clean and professional, might be another $300.

Another question that always arises in my travels concerns jingles. Again, I am going to give you the same advice: hire local talent.

But my logic is somewhat different here. To fully explain myself, let's look at the reality of jingle use in America today. Here is the usual sequence of events. First, someone, a radio station, cable system or TV station hosts

"JG" (Jingle Gypsy) for a week or so. The JG then visits a bunch of clients and comes up with jingle ideas and sells them in conjunction with a package of ads that must run on the host station. So far, so good, as the JGs are usually fine people and have good syndicated stuff from which to choose—nice, snappy, syndicated tunes, good syndicated lyrics and syndicated punch lines that will stick in your head.

I sure hope you noted my overuse of the word "syndicated." JGs' jingles are all coming from some master library or production house and being adapted to your business. They are usually not customized for you. I'm not saying that's a horrific crime. Many of them end up working just fine. I'm saying there is a better way.

The better way is to have your jingle truly custom-made for your business. You then save a lot of money with no contract with anyone. You do not need to spend $3,000, $4,000 or more on your jingle. And you don't need to be stuck with a contract that forces you to commit thousands more in advertising to the station or cable system that hosts the JG.

Here is how you get your jingle for $300 to $500 dollars, have it truly custom-made for your business and maintain the freedom to run it anywhere you choose in your market:

Hire local talent.

The local music store can refer you to a dozen singers who will gladly arrange and sing your jingle for you for a few bucks and the glory of being on the air. All you have to do is come up with the punch line, or at least a vision of what you want to convey in the punch line, so they can invent it for you.

Afraid you can't find the idea for the punch line? Go back to chapter two and re-do your detective work to settle on the one purpose or one singular magic wand wish for your advertising. That is usually the punch line.

Let's look at our jeweler from Rochester. He did his detective work. He realized he was perceived as high priced when in fact, he had a huge advantage with lower costs downtown. My suggestion for a punch line for a jingle would be "Diamonds cost less downnnntownnnn." If we air that constantly, it becomes stuck in the brains of every woman in the market. Now she has to at least consider giving his store a try, because her brain is singing, "Diamonds cost less downnnntownnnn."

What about all the other lyrics, the 60 seconds of singing you get with the syndicators? The six versions in country style, folk style, rap style, oldies style, dance style and Indonesian style orchestration? Forget it. You don't need all that stuff. In fact, anything other than the one tagline, one hook line or one punch line is a waste and will soon be abandoned by you anyway. The real purpose of your jingle is to take a hook line and embed it in the brains of the audience.

Here is some proof of this concept. It works the same way in commercial song writing. You all know the hook lines to at least a million tunes, but I bet you cannot sing the entire lyrics and all verses to more than one or two. My daughter-in-law is the star American Pie singer at wedding parties. Properly fueled with the right beverages she can sing it from start to finish flawlessly. All the words, all the verses. But ask her to do the same to a song like Stairway to Heaven and the best she, or you, or I, or most anyone can do is the punch line ……and I'm climbing a stairwayyyyy to Heavvennnn.

After your local songster does a great five-second or so tagline, you now have the obligation to run it in every ad every time you are on the air. At some point, every bride-to-be has your punch line memorized. You have become Big Brother and have forced her to memorize your punch line. Now when it becomes her turn to look for an engagement ring, a little tune kicks off in her head and it is exactly the tune you chose: "Diamonds cost less downnnntownnnn."

WHAT ABOUT

TOMORROW?

Thus, I end my rules. I have hopefully provided stimulating and thought-provoking analysis of how you should advertise. In the dynamic, ever-changing business world, you need to employ tactics that work. In just the last decade think of the changes that have occurred:

The increase in the number of radio stations.

The decrease in daily newspaper readership.

The increase in cable channels and satellite TV.

The decrease in tolerance for the ensuing increase in commercial messages.

The increase in new broadcast TV networks like Fox, The C/W, etc.

The decrease in radio audiences at home in the morning.

The increase in local TV dominance at home in the mornings.

The decrease in radio listening by those under 25.

The increase of music being heard on iPods by those under 25.

The decrease in radio station audiences listening in cars.

The increase of satellite radio audiences and cell phones in cars.

The decrease in market share of any ABC/CBS/NBC stations.

The increase of market share on cable.

The decrease in effectiveness of the strategy of "media mix."

The increase in the effectiveness of the strategy of "concentration."

The decrease by young people in the use of large, fixed electronic devices.

The increase by young people in the use of tiny, mobile, handheld devices.

It truly has been a sea of change. But wait. Embedded in the midst of that ocean another tidal wave of change is building that will totally rewrite the entire dynamic of the advertising market.

I speak, of course, of the Internet. Its impact is already huge. News dissemination, shopping and practically all forms of commerce have been impacted. I'm just not sure how the Internet will affect local advertising or the use of my 14 Rules in the future. One thing that is certain is that there will be some effect. How to prepare for those effects?

Pay attention and re-evaluate your marketing strategy twice a year. Remember the questions we asked back in chapter three with Big Bob and his fireworks store? I would suggest you ask them at least once every six months. It's all changing that fast. You simply cannot afford to experiment and hope for that magic bullet, that killer ad. The competition is too great and the cost too high.

Finally, I'd like to attach some ideas for you to use to measure the results you get from your advertising.

MEASURING RESULTS

1- THE EAR METER

This is the least reliable of all measures. Basically the customer is asked, "How did you hear about us?" Answers will range from the reasonable to the absurd. Answers will include media being used and media not being used. To make the Ear Meter work, you must include something in the commercial that generates comments—for example, using the owner in the ad.

2- THE SALES METER

This is a very reliable measure but it cannot be reviewed alone as it appears in your sales reports. To make the Sales Meter work, you must measure sales over a period of time and then factor in all outside influences, including market statistics, the sales of the competitors, seasonal variances, plus any internal issues you have with product, services and staff. A success may well be an increase in sales, or holding a sales loss to 2 percent in an environment where everyone else is down 8 percent.

In some competitive categories, data exists to allow you to calculate your gain or loss of share of sales in a market. Auto dealers all have this data. If a Ford dealer goes from a 24 percent share of Ford sales to 30 percent in the local market, that is a win. Your state usually reports tax dollars collected in certain categories like furniture. If a furniture store pays an increasing share of total tax collected, they are selling a greater share of the furniture. That is a win. Very often, the manufacturer's rep who calls on your store knows who has what for market share.

3 - THE BRAND METER

This is a great survey you can conduct yourself. Survey at random about 100 people who represent the target demographic. Your goal is to discover where you are positioned in the brain of the consumer. You would do this before a campaign runs, then again after it runs and measure the changes. If you do this yourself, you must buy and read <u>Positioning the Battle for Your Mind</u> by Reis and Trout. Here is a sample for a law firm:

If I ask you to give me the names of several law firms, what names come to your mind?

This will give you the relative strength of your position in the general category of law. Now we want to see where they stand in specific areas:

- What is the biggest law firm?
- What is the most expensive?
- What has the best lawyers?

Which law firm would you consider for advice on:
- Buying a home?
- Retirement planning?
- A car accident?
- A very serious injury claim?
- Bankruptcy?
- A drunken driving charge?

Finally, we want to know what image, if any, you have in the mind of the average Joe.

- What comes to your mind when I mention some names like law firm A, law firm B (your firm), or law firm C?

4 - THE MEDIA METER

This is a very reliable way to be sure you are advertising to the right people and using the right media. Ideally, the Media Meter would become a routine part of your business to build a database over time. Try using these Media Survey Questions (customize for the particular business):

1. Have you ever purchased from us in the past?

YES/NO

- If yes, how often?

2. Did you check the newspaper prior to shopping?
YES/NO

- If yes, which publication?

a. Local daily paper

b. Nearby daily paper

c. Local shopper

d. Other

3. Do you subscribe to the daily newspaper? YES/NO

- If yes, do you subscribe DAILY or just SUNDAY?
- On a typical weekday, how many minutes do you spend reading the paper?
- On a typical Sunday how many minutes do you spend reading the paper?

4. What are your three favorite radio stations or radio personalities?

5. When you wake up in the morning, do you turn on the TV? YES/NO

- If yes, what do you usually watch?

6. For the local news during the day and at night, what local TV station do you usually watch?

7. What are your favorite programs on television during the daytime on your local TV stations?

8. What are your three favorite programs on television at night on your local TV stations?

9. Do you subscribe to cable or satellite TV? If yes to one, what time of day to you usually watch cable or satellite? MORNING/DAYTIME/NIGHT/OVERNIGHT

10. What are your three favorite networks or shows on cable or satellite during the day? Your three favorite at night?

11. If you received five pieces of direct mail in your mailbox in any one day, how many of those will you usually read?

12. Did you use the Internet to find our store or research our services? YES/NO

Note: Ideally the client will fill in some estimates on the customer demographics, for example:

Age_____ Sex_____ Blue Collar_____ White Collar_____

Zip Code_____Income_____ Etc_____.

5 - THE WEB METER

Here is where we see the real future of measurable results. The web provides you the ultimate in accountability. Consider your local media as you would a traffic cop at a busy intersection. Local media can direct traffic to your web site, and there it can be measured and counted.

If increased web hits are your goal, run your media to direct traffic to your web site and count the increases in web activity.

If you want to stake your future on your web site, use your local media to claim a position as the best web site in your category. For example, a real estate agent might claim to have the "best web site on the planet for home buyers." Or a used car dealer might stake out a position via local media as "the best used car web site for those who want low-mileage, late-model import cars."

Personally, I see this as the future for those who want measurability. But to do it right, you must stay focused on a message that says, "visit our web site" and nothing else.

Remember, when all the dust settles, the point of this book remains the same: It's all about measurable results, and I really hope I help you get them!